W9-CCQ-635

'05

THE ART OF LYING

THE ART
OF LYING

KAZUO SAKAI, M.D.
NAKANA IDE

TRANSLATED BY
Sara Aoyama

RED BRICK PRESS
New York

Copyright © 1998 by Hatherleigh Press
Original title Uso no kenkyū Copyright © Sakai Kazuo
Originally published in Japan in 1996
by FOUR U (Publishing) Co., Ltd.

All rights reserved. No part of this book may be reproduced
in any form or by any means, electronic or mechanical,
including photocopying, recording, or by any information
storage and retrieval system, without permission in writing
from the publisher.

Red Brick Press
An Independent Imprint of Hatherleigh Press
1114 First Avenue, Suite 500
New York, NY 10021
1-800-367-2550
www.hatherleigh.com

Printed in Canada

This edition is printed on acid-free paper that meets the
American National Standards Institute z39-48 Standard.

Library of Congress Cataloging-in-Publication Data
Sakai, Kazuo, 1951–
[Uso no kenkyū. English]
The art of lying–[Uso no kenkyū] / Kazuo Sakai, Nakana Ide. :
translated by Sara Aoyama.
p. cm.
ISBN 1-886330-91-3 (alk.. paper)
1. Truthfulness and Falsehood.   I. Ide, Nakana, 1945 –
II. Title.
BJ1428.J3S2513   1998
177' . 3–dc21   98-10064
CIP

All Red Brick Press titles are available for bulk purchase,
special promotions, and premiums. For more information,
please contact the manager of our Special Sales Department
at 1-800-367-2550.
Designed by DC Designs

10 9 8 7 6 5 4 3 2 1

CONTENTS

FOREWORD

ONE OF THE LAST THINGS I expected to be writing was a foreword to a book that in any way advocated lying. After all, I was taught early on that not being truthful was just plain wrong. That's not to imply that I never engaged in a prevarication, but I never did so without some sense of discomfort, to say the least. Therefore, I began to read *The Art of Lying* with some trepidation. It was when I reached the part where the author pointed out that a well-established technique of medical investigation consistently involves lying that I reacted with surprise and sudden recognition....an "of course!" response. I've done a fair amount of clinical research in my career. I know the importance of comparing a new medical treatment with a placebo to determine its effectiveness. Everyone involved in the experiment knows that some patients are getting the active drug while others are getting what amounts to a sugar pill, but the patients are more or less told that they are all getting a true medication. In this way, the power of suggestion by the mere act of taking a pill can be assessed and weighed into the evaluation of whether the new compound is or is not significantly useful. In other words, any of us who carry out such investigations are essentially lying, using the placebo lie for a valuable purpose, to be sure, but lying nonetheless.

So I decided to interrupt my reading to go to my thesaurus. There I discovered a long list of nouns and verbs that were closely aligned to "lie"...to invent, distort, fabricate, equivocate, falsify, or fib; mendacity, untruth, prevarication, *fiction*; to dodge, hedge, side-step, pussyfoot, and (a word I've never encountered before) tergiversate. I was at once struck by the fact that lying often involves behavior, not just verbalization. You can live a lie as easily as speaking one. Avoiding the truth can be categorized as lying no less than actively telling an untruth. One can even see a certain amount of creativity or imagination involved, in such terms as invention and fiction.

And this procedure alerted me to another dimension of lying. When you read a novel or see a film, you know that it's not a true story; you're told this right on the cover of the book —*A Novel by So-and-So* —and so there is really no deception involved. It's when you don't know that it's a story that a betrayal of the integrity of communication takes place.

Another point. Does the end justify the means? I was taught it does not; I still believe this. So, if lying is essentially wrong, how does one justify using a placebo in research or, in the rather simple example I remember from my ethics course in college, telling a man who has come to your house to injure or even kill your father that your father is not at home, completing the sentence silently to yourself (my father is not at home *to you*). Is it possible that there is a valid place for the lie in human interactions? If so, there can be a place for a book such as *The Art of Lying* that presents the subject in a more positive, even at times admirable, light.

Must you tell every dying patient that he or she is dying in so many words? Are you justified in lying when you side-step giving bad news to someone because you think they can't handle it right now? Should you feel comfortable lying to embellish a true story you're telling someone to emphasize a point or make it more interesting or humorous? Where do you draw the line? I would have been happier had Dr. Sakai explored these ethical issues in greater depth. But I'm confident readers can do so for themselves.

I would have been happier as well had the author afforded many more examples of shading the truth, so to speak, in situations other than man-woman relationships. Love relationships are perhaps the most common situations in which lying occurs, but they are also the place where honesty and fidelity are most called for. Let's not forget that we encounter lying in many other circumstances too. The business lie. The money lie. The political lie. And in each one of these one must consider whether they are with or without justification and how much good or how much damage they do.

A final thought that was sparked by my reading: how do we react when we catch someone else in a lie? Again it depends on what our relationship with the person who has fibbed to us is, the seriousness of the falsification, and, of course, the net effect. Was the purpose of the lie to avoid conflict, to keep us from being unnecessarily hurt, to deceive, to protect the interests of the liar? Do we hold it against that person forever or do we forgive? Do we take it as a warning sign that the relationship should probably not continue? Do we understand that the truth avoided or the untruth spoken was an effort to protect us in some way?

It is prudent to distinguish between the one who tells the lie, the so-called "liar," and the act of lying itself. A lie does not necessarily a liar make. I remember a mother and her teenage son who consulted with me in an effort to improve their relationship. He had denied taking twenty dollars from her wallet when, in fact, he had. The mother repeatedly and harshly referred to her son as a "liar." In response, he bristled, cried a little, and grew more sullen. I gently but pointedly admonished her for using the word "liar" in that way. "Your son did tell you a lie," I agreed. "In a minute, I'll ask him to tell us why he felt the need to do so. But for future reference, if you can avoid attacking his self-respect by using the word liar, if we can deal with the behavior itself, we can take some of the sting out of this conversation and move toward some real resolution here."

Lying. Distorting. Fabricating. White lies and serious lies. Dodging. Pussyfooting. Deceiving. Certainly these behaviors are part and parcel of the human experience. Certainly truth, not falsehood, is the root of genuine relatedness. But, as the author suggests, there may well be a constructive element in certain kinds of fabrication. After all, doesn't optimism often involve fabrication? And kindness, at times. And love?

If it is not already apparent, I must point out that I do take exception to some of the points Dr. Sakai makes. This is one reason I found it thought-provoking. For the western reader, he gives us new, valuable, and sometimes delightful insights into Japanese culture.

Frederic Flach, M.D.

TRANSLATOR'S NOTE

*T*he *Art of Lying* was originally written by a Japanese psychiatrist, as a book designed to appeal to the average Japanese reader. The Japanese people, as a nation, are voracious readers, as evidenced by the large number of bookstores and the large variety of periodicals readily available. Each year, more and more books from the West are translated into Japanese, providing excellent exposure to Western writing. In contrast, we English readers rarely get a chance to see what the average Japanese person is reading at home. One reason why there are so few Japanese books translated into Western languages is because much of the meaning conveyed through the written word in Japanese is found in the characters, which evolved from pictographs. The picture and the image it evokes are difficult to represent in our Western writing system.

The ideas of "psychology" and "self-exploration" are still very new to the Japanese people. The whole notion of counseling holds a certain amount of stigma for the general population. In many ways, the samurai spirit still prevails, and if you have some sort of problem in your life, you are expected to deal with it quietly and privately. The influx of Western media—movies, books, television—has focused some amount of attention on newer ideas such as "encounter groups" and therapy, and you will see these ideas reflected in this book.

The attitudes in this book may seem very foreign to you. Many Western readers may find the portrayal of women offensive. It is my firm opinion that most Japanese women of the same generation as the author would NOT find this book offensive. But Japan is a constantly changing society, and while no one wants to rock the boat too rapidly, there is evidence that the younger generation may develop a different way of looking at things. Women in Japan may appear to have little power, but in truth it is most often the woman who has the economic power in the household. This is a little-known fact that most women keep very quiet. This is one kind of "lie" that the author does not directly address, but his theory on the use of lies is certainly applicable here. Japanese men often help out with the housework, but unlike many American men, who will boast about how much they do around the house, a Japanese man will not want to admit that he takes on this less-than-manly role. Here is yet another kind of "lie" that exists in Japan. One of the biggest lies in Japan is that of the "helplessness" and "cute femininity" of women, who are actually as a group quite powerful in some arenas. Nonetheless, workplace issues lag far behind in equality and any examples given in this book are accurate portrayals of the current status of women.

I would like to reiterate that this book was written for a Japanese audience, which is culturally miles apart from a Western audience. The Japanese are not linear thinkers, and as evidenced in Japanese literature, they are quite satisfied to provoke thought rather than draw conclusions. Many of the ideas Dr. Sakai presents are new to the Japanese people, and these ideas serve to enhance the practicality of this Japanese self-help book. To the Western reader it may serve as a self-help book or perhaps more importantly as a window to both Japanese contemporary culture and an overview of the role of psychology in Japan today.

Sara Aoyama

Preface
AN INVITATION
TO LYING

The nineteenth-century philosopher and poet Ralph Waldo Emerson said that "a gentleman never tells a lie." Westerners, and above all Americans, believe that telling a lie is a most abhorrent immoral act. This is a reflection of logic in the dogma of Christianity, and if a person is called a "liar" then it is as if his character has been besmirched. In some cases being called a liar is considered to be the ultimate insult, and has even lead to duels.

When we consider what a lie is in our own country, we can look at old sayings such as "Telling a lie is the first step on the road of crime" or "If you tell a lie you will go to hell." We too seem to adhere to a belief system that strictly admonishes for telling a lie. But on the other hand, we also have such sayings as "A lie is sometimes expedient" and "You have to lie to get ahead in the world." Paradoxically, this seems to suggest that there is evidence that a lie may be a useful thing. Our cultural sensibilities are quite different from those of the West, and it is no exaggeration to say that there is a stronger basis for the lie to flourish in the Eastern sense of daily life.

Since the time we became aware of our surroundings, we have learned to watch the face of an adult. If we have a sense that we will be scolded, we automatically tell a lie to avoid discomfort. This is not something that is taught to us, but more of an instinct toward self-protection. An old fashioned interpretation might be that human beings have an innate sense of either evil or good. These two are always battling each other, but in many cases it seems that evil wins out.

Because of this, parents and school teachers are always saying to children that "it is wrong to tell a lie." In spite of that, the majority of children are aware that these words are only surface-level. They know that parents and teachers, as well as all adults, tell lies and they can understand that sometimes a lie actually helps improve a situation.

In actuality, there are many cases in which it is better to *not* tell the truth than to tell a lie. If you grew up thinking that "honesty is the greatest virtue," then you may have a hard time grasping this. When it is said that a person has a good understanding of the ins and outs of life, you can be pretty sure this person is practiced at lying. A good lie is like the spice we use when cooking. It improves the flavor and adds variety to the enjoyment of life—it's an essential ingredient.

Contrary to what our parents and teachers have taught us, then, people who can tell lies well often have deeper and more interesting lives. There are many cases in which lies are very successful. In general, when you compare men's lying to women's, women are often making up trivial little lies, whereas men tend to tell really elaborate lies about two or three times a year.

In spite of this, it is sometimes difficult in everyday life to tell a good or skillful lie. Just like telling jokes, it is necessary to have a certain amount of wit and sense.

When we wrote this book, we did not plan to have Chapter 8. But then we decided to add some examples of how to tell a lie skillfully. We hope that whether you are a gentleman or a lady that these lies will be useful to you and help all of our readers lie effectively so that you can enjoy life with even more color and richness.

Ide Nakana

THE ART OF LYING

Chapter 1
WHY DO
PEOPLE LIE?

ONLY HUMANS LIE FOR FUN

The Dutch cultural historian Huizinga calls human beings *Homo ludicer* or "playful being." Among all the many established ways of categorizing human beings—*Homo sapiens* ("thinking being") and *Homo fabrico* ("making being")— this one strikes me as the most refreshing and precise definition of mankind.

Still, in my opinion, human beings are *Homo mendosus* or "lying being."

Human beings are not the only living creature with the ability to "lie." Chameleons and some insects have this ability as well, but their forms of camouflage are very limited. There is usually just one pattern to their ability to deceive.

Compared to these creatures, the lie of the human being has a very complicated structure. This is not because we use the spoken word to lie, but rather due to the fact that we have a foundation to use a lie or deceit in a playful manner.

Humans often use lies to trick people, or as a way to bring about financial gain or some greater good. (One example would be the "sting" operation used by the FBI in America to catch a criminal in the act.) But most of the lies that we ordinary people use daily have an element of play to them.

For example, look at most current novels and plays. This kind of fiction is meant to be created by human beings; it's a fantasy world to be enjoyed or to provide suspense or entertainment. Even though it is made up, nobody cries out: "It's all a sham!" Likewise, it is only those people with a healthy psyche that are able to enjoy a lie for what it is: a lie. The same can be said about lies in everyday life.

If we humans were only to speak the truth, our lives would become extremely awkward. If we didn't exchange pleasantries and flattery to grease the social wheel, jealousy and resentment would bubble up and relations between people would fail to go smoothly.

And if we were unable to tell an occasional lie to ourselves, we might find ourselves falling into despair at our very existence.

Take the example of the child who doesn't want to go to school, because "All my friends pick on me." If that child looks hard at the real reason for the bullying, he may feel he has no choice but to commit suicide. But, instead, a child will cleverly fool himself: "My stomach hurts so I can't go to school." He unconsciously uses this as a way to avoid ridicule. And at least for one day that child is able to escape his predicament.

This is one example of what's known as a "defense mechanism" at work. If you are able to lie to yourself successfully, then you need not get depressed, or go crazy, and you can go on with your life. You could call this self-deception, but I prefer to call it a kind of innate instinct that a human being must develop in order to stay alive.

A lie—or deception—is an important component in daily human life. It may sound extreme, but most of us are able to carve our niche in society and make a life for ourselves because of our ability to lie. In fact, it is no exaggeration to say that human society is built upon lies on a magnificent scale.

The French existentialist philosopher Jean-Paul Sartre says, "Imagination leads the world." Rephrasing that I will venture to say, "Lies lead the world." There is no doubt in my mind that people should feel at liberty to tell lies that serve to bring about happiness.

THE USE OF DELIBERATE AND INTENTIONAL LIES

There are two kinds of people who lie.

First are those people who, without being aware of it themselves, just find themselves telling a lie. Most lies in this category are made to cover up a weak point. For example, you tell a lie that you have a lover to impress others, when you really don't.

But this kind of lie is just a temporary stopgap. When you tell this lie, you may have a brief feeling of satisfaction, but no matter how many times you say it, your real situation will not change for the better. The only thing you can gain is a feeling of regret.

However, a deliberate, planned-out lie can have some unexpected good effect. For example, just a very small lie may be the solution to smoothing over a complicated relationship.

There is a tendency not to tell a lie to people who have a lot of influence or power over you. You rarely tell a lie to a superior at work, or to a partner whom you love with all your heart. Lies to superiors are more likely made when you have little respect for them, and lies to lovers are generally made when you aren't really in love.

So, if a relationship in your life is not going well, but this is a person that you have never lied to in the past, I recommend that you boldly try telling a lie.

I'm not saying you should tell a big lie; a very small lie will do. When you tell this lie, the important thing is to observe very carefully the reaction you get.

For example, let's imagine that you have a boss at work whom you trust very much. But, you are unable to gauge the degree of trust your boss has towards you.

You could try a little lie out, such as "This project that you've asked me to do—I'm afraid it may be too difficult for me to handle." Of course, if you do this at a time when you are involved with a very important task, your value as an employee could be undermined. So it's important to try this kind of lie when you are working on something that is not so urgent or important.

How will your boss react to your words?

He could respond with, "I see. Well, I'll get someone else to handle it then." Or, he may say, "I disagree. You are definitely up to the challenge." Either way, if you observe carefully you will be able to know objectively just what he thinks of your ability. Furthermore, since this is a lie you have manufactured, there is the added merit that you should be able to distance yourself from his response and observe things very coolly and calmly.

The same kind of thing can be done in a relationship between a man and a woman. You may say to your partner, whom you have been with for many years, but have yet to receive any commitment, "By the way, there is some talk of my doing a *omiai*[1] soon." With the right timing, even an old-fashioned lie like this can have some good results.

If your partner shows little reaction to these words and says something like, "That's a good idea," then it may be the impetus you need to break off the relationship!

A FEELING OF RELEASE

When you tell a lie, it's said, your heart beats a little faster. The same is thought to be true when you are hiding a secret: you become nervous and agitated.

But actually, the opposite is true. A person keeping a secret is often more mentally in control. Everybody in the world has one or two things they want to hide from others. Or we may have many things that we are hiding. It may be a romantic affair that we have fallen into, or something top secret at work. No matter what it is, it is necessary to tell lies to maintain the secrecy. A person who cannot tell a lie well often cannot keep a secret.

In order to go on with my explanation from here,

---

[1] An omiai is a kind of prospective match which would lead to marriage. Traditionally one would attend such a meeting and then it would lead quickly to marriage, but in modern Japan the omiai meeting has less formality to it and is almost similar to a blind date. Before the initial meeting, the two people may exchange photos and "resumes" to make sure that

it is first necessary to look at the case of a person who is mentally unstable.

In most cases, a patient with mental illness can not lie very well. People suffering from mental illness, and in particular schizophrenia, are unable to deceive others. We can also say that they are unable to hide a secret for any amount of time as well. This is because they have problems with mental control and accuracy. They are unable to distinguish between a lie and the truth.

In order to keep a secret it is necessary to accurately distinguish within your mind complex lies and the truth. In addition, a huge amount of effort is required to translate these lies successfully into words. A secret must be kept deep within one's heart and the ability to freely manipulate the truth and lies is thus imperative.

But if you were instead to try to deliberately keep a secret to yourself, you would have to concentrate on the secret in your heart and maintain a flexible coping attitude towards the outside world. Just as you can make your fingers more flexible through

they even want to meet. Either party may reject the other at any time. The go-between plays an important role in the omiai and may be a relative or a superior at work. It is said that up to 40% of marriages in Japan are still "omiai" marriages, in contrast to "love marriages" where the couple meets without the aid of a go-between. Young people in Japan may experience a number of omiai meetings before finding an acceptable marriage partner.

training them, you can also train yourself to be more mentally flexible.

You can see some examples of this in the European secret societies or the Japanese new religions.[2]

In order to gain entrance to a secret society, new inductees often attend a ceremony where certain secrets are imparted to them. These secrets may never ever be told to any outsiders—new inductees must swear never to reveal them. In the Japanese new religions, a high ranking instructor reveals some secret words and phrases and then trains newcomers in how to keep them secret.

In both of these cases, secrets are created deliberately. This is an example of a group using secrets to gain the loyalty of each member of that group.

A healthy psyche is not entirely based on the ability to tell the truth. A healthy psyche includes the ability to skillfully control the use of lies *and* the truth.

In that respect, it is absolutely necessary for your own healthy psyche to keep some secrets in your heart that are yours and yours alone.

---

[2] "New religions" in Japan run the gauntlet from innocuous all the way up to cult-like in their organization. The Aum Sect, known for their subway bombings, is one example of a "new religion."

WORRYING, CONFLICT AND LIES

If you can't tell a lie, you cannot escape from worrying and conflict. It is often mistakenly thought that honesty and objectivity are one and the same.

Some strange results appeared when we compared the results of psychological tests given to a group of patients at a psychiatric hospital with results from the same tests given to a group of junior college students. The students tested had a lower personality integration score and rate of development than the patients at the clinic. A random selection of the scores of ten members of each group were shown to a European psychiatrist for analysis. He concluded that, indeed, the scores of the students showed more abnormalities.

At first, we believed that perhaps the level of the college was the problem, and theorized that if the same test was given to higher-level college students, then the results would be improved. But, whether the test was taken by students at private universities or at more elite national universities, there was no significant change in the results. At the very least, academic ability seems unrelated to personality integration and development.

In that case, why is it that the results of psychological tests (projection) of patients coming to the clinic are so good? That is due to the fact that these patients have reached the level where they are "worrying."

There is a word called "non-reactive." Most students these days are good examples of "non-reactive beings," meaning, they worry less. People who worry are honest and sincere to themselves and others. They are people who cannot tell a lie. In that respect, we often say they are very "human."

However, in almost all cases, people who worry have extremely low objectivity. To be honest and to not lie is, in one respect, being very subjective (personal) and looking at and judging things only from your own point of view.

It is difficult for people who worry to reach the psychological state of "conflict." Before you reach this state of "conflict," it is necessary that you be able to see your own problems. Conflict occurs when there is a feeling of having resistance, being highly objective, and you find that your ability and personality are not in synch with your circumstances, causing you to be more aware of your problems.

Conflict has significance, but worrying has almost no value at all. The more honest a person who is plagued by worries is, the more chance there is that this person will be a worrier all his or her life. And worriers are often chronically down in the dumps.

On the other hand, people in conflict are in danger of finally rupturing. A person who is unable to choose between solution A, B, or C is likely to experience extreme depression. This is also the type of person who may commit suicide.

What these people lack is the ability to tell a small lie, to be a little more flexible in their moral outlook on the world.

Try this little exercise: in a case where you would normally say no very honestly, try saying yes, or "that sounds interesting." If you can say the opposite of what you are really thinking for a period of one month, you will find that what other people think of you will change dramatically. More importantly, the way you yourself see the world will undergo a complete change.

It is very difficult to change one's personality. But to take on a more relaxed and positive attitude towards lying and keep on with it is something anyone can do.

Worrying and conflict both come from not being able to separate from oneself, and from being too attached to one's problems. If this is the case, then why not try turning the tables in your relationship between your self and your surroundings? Disengage a little. If you can do this, you will be able to gain a little distance and some perspective on your problems.

If you find it impossible to "tell lies for one month" at least try to tell three *constructive* lies during the next few weeks. Whether it be to your lover, husband or wife, or colleague, the results will be the same. Their estimation of you will change and the way you feel will change as well.

Sometimes we have the urge to run away from a problem. At this time you should also try telling a constructive lie. There may be some very unexpected benefits from skipping an important meeting at work. If you tell a constructive lie, people will not guess that you are just skipping out on work, and you will feel easier about it.

It is a fact that most of the people who come to my clinic are serious, troubled people whose personalities make it hard for them to tell a lie. Unfortunately, it's very difficult to recommend to them that they "go out and tell a constructive lie." They'd quickly be thinking, "What kind of nutty doctor is this?" This is because they come to my clinic believing that sincerity is all-important and they must solve their own problems within the clear limits of sincerity.

When You Can't Lie to Yourself

A human heart is a convenient thing. A healthy person is able to accept and deal with most of the changes in their environment. For example, even if there is a small amount of psychological conflict or trouble, a healthy person can overcome this by speaking to themselves and working it through in their minds for the better; they have the strength to overcome these problems.

However, when the conflict is too strong, or when they lack the ability to adapt within their own heart and mind, it may be impossible to work their problems out.

There was an incident recently involving a woman who appeared to be in her thirties. The police found her wandering around in the snow fields in the suburbs. When they questioned her, they were unable to learn anything about her. She was unable to provide any kind of satisfactory answers to questions of where she lived, where she was born, her work or age and even what her name was. Even by looking through her belongings they were unable to confirm her identity. Frustrated, the police ended up taking her to the hospital.

At the hospital, they attempted a variety of treatments, but they made little significant progress. As a last resort, the doctors decided to use sodium pentithal, a kind of anesthetic that is also used around the world by scientists and authorities as a truth serum. (You may have seen scenes in spy thrillers in which someone is strapped into a chair, given an injection by a secret agent, and then suddenly spills out everything. That is the kind of drug that was used here.)

The sodium pentithal served as a catalyst to free

this woman from her mental suppression. In a state of semi-consciousness she was able to respond to the doctor's questions. As a result, they finally learned that she was a 28-year-old civil servant who lived over 300 kilometers away from the town where she was found.

Right before she disappeared, she had become engaged to a man whom she really did not like. The people around her refused to acknowledge her feelings and circumstances, and did not support her. She was trapped into a situation in which she would soon be forced to marry the man.

At that point, she abandoned her home and workplace and chose to escape to an unknown town. No matter how unwilling she was to marry this man, she was also unable to go against the wishes of her family, whom she loved and respected, by openly refusing him. She lied to her parents regarding her true feelings about the marriage and was unable to break away from her fiancé. At that point, her subconscious, instead of her conscious self, automatically took over to protect herself from the dilemma inside her heart.

This phenomenon is called "psychogenic flight." It happens in today's stressful world to middle-aged men, and people in responsible positions. They want to escape from their workplaces but feel unable to do so due to their societal obligations. This conflict buries their memory of themselves and their feelings of responsibility deep down in the bogs of their consciousness.

There are many different kinds of memory loss, but when a person totally loses their past it is called "full life amnesia." When a human being faces a conflict within their heart they are unable to accept, they have deep within them a formidable power to erase their entire identity.

How a Lie Can Cure an Illness

Even in the field of medicine, there are famous cases of lies.

Placebos were originally used for scientific experimentation in order to see if a new medication really did have an effect. If it is an oral medication then lactose or starch is used; if it is an injection, then a saline solution is used. The color, shape, flavor, etc., are designed to be identical to the original medicine and then it is given to the patient. Another group of patients is given the real medication, and by comparing the effects for the two groups, scientists are able to view objectively the efficacy of the drug.

However, interestingly enough, there have been cases where starch pills (which have no healing power whatsoever) have had a beneficial effect, even causing an illness to be cured! This kind of phenomenon is called "the placebo effect." In my field of psychiatry, the placebo effect can often be observed in the treatment of insomnia: I have often prescribed a placebo in the form of a vitamin to treat this disorder. And I have seen even a severe case of insomnia be cured with it.

Naturally, when a placebo is used, the patient must be totally unaware of its use. Often, a "double blind test" is done, meaning even the doctor remains unaware of which drug is the placebo. In any case, when the drug is given to the patient, the doctor tells the patient something reassuring such as, "This medication will cure your problem." Thus, the patient believes, "Yes, if I take this I will feel better." It is this *conviction* that cures the disorder or disease.

Let's analyze this process from a medical point of view.

The patient who has received this medication is first of all left with the assurance that "my illness will be cured with this medication." That emotion serves to trigger the immune system, which then heightens the power of resistance to the illness. In other words, since this positive feeling has an influence on the physiological level, a placebo truly *can* cure an illness. In direct opposition to this is a phenomenon called "iatrogenic disease."

In the broadest sense of the term, iatrogenic disease can be caused by simple mistakes made by the doctor, but more often it is provoked by a doctor's bad attitude towards a patient. For example, a doctor fails to provide a detailed explanation of the patient's illness, and just shakes his head silently. The patient, observing this, thinks to himself, "It must be something really bad." This causes his symptoms to worsen.

Among cancer researchers, there are those who say that the cause of cancer in half of the cases can be linked to psychological stress. "If that wasn't the case, then how can you explain the fact that among people exposed to cancer-causing substances, some of them get cancer and some of them don't?"

There is a saying that "illness comes from within oneself." Although having an illness should never be considered the fault of the patient, at times his recovery will be helped by his belief that "I will get better. I know I will get well." And in order to help the patient believe that he will recover, a small lie will often be effective.

LIES TO DISCOVER HIDDEN TALENTS

One way to help a person change is through participation in an "encounter group." In an encounter group, a number of people who don't know each other meet together in kind of a training session for the purposes of self improvement. Broadly speaking, there are two kinds of encounter groups—structured and unstructured.

I will not try to describe an encounter group in detail here, but one of the methods that is used in a structured group is having members take turns extolling the strong points of other members.

In the beginning, the strong points that could obviously be noted in that person are expressed. But when it comes to the second round, or even the third round, it becomes difficult to find anything positive to say about a person that one really doesn't know all that well. Inevitably, words that have been just thought up on the spur of the moment and have no real bearing on the truth start to come out.

If this kind of obvious flattery were aimed at someone in real life, that person might find it hard to believe and might even become insulted. But under the guise of an encounter session, the person to whom these words are directed finds himself feeling better and better rather than getting angry. And, by the time the session is over, he finds himself filled with confidence.

Of course, deep down in the bottom of his heart he knows that the people around him at this session are probably just flattering him. But, even knowing this, his confidence improves and even upon returning to the real world he is able to continue feeling confident for some time.

In the field of sports there are also cases where lying to yourself can help get better results. One example is in shooting—a field where the power of concentration is particularly important. Your whole focus is upon a tiny target far away on which a bullet must be aimed with machine-like precision in order to hit it. Many competitors in this sport use image training before their competition. They imagine that they have achieved a perfect score by shooting every single one of their bullets directly into the exact center of the target.

It is almost impossible for a person to achieve a perfect score when shooting, so in some sense this is really telling a lie. However, the results of this kind of image training are absolute. Players who use this method beforehand are extremely calm and in competition they improve their scores significantly.

This is just another way that lying to yourself can help you create confidence in yourself.

And, depending on how creatively you use a lie, it can also be the impetus towards finding hidden abilities in yourself.

Chapter 2
TRY TELLING A LIE TO YOURSELF

THE WORLD OF LIES IS THE REAL WORLD

It is probably a sign that I am getting on in years to say this, but the truth is that when I observe young people today, many of them strike me as lacking in self confidence. They have no real idea of what they want to do, and are unable to see their own true self. No matter how many experiences they collect, they lack the conviction that "this is the path that I want to take." There has been a marked increase recently of young people like this among the patients at my clinic.

This phenomenon is vividly presented in the American psychologist Dan Kiley's best seller, *The Peter Pan Syndrome* as well as in the classic text by Eric Erikson called *Moratorium*. We can try to severely admonish these kind of young people and tell them to "hurry up and grow up" or "find your place in life." But studies show it does no good at all. They make no attempt to find any other world other than their own, and even though they are desperate to be loved themselves, they refuse to make the effort to love others.

Just like the character of Peter Pan, some people need a Wendy to take care of everything. The tendency of males to think they are superior to women, who they assume should be subordinate to men, is also a common trait here. In many cases I believe this tendency is due to an excessive amount of interference by the parents.

How should we treat this kind of young person? If by some chance, you know a young person like this, and if they are already over the age of twenty, you may have no choice but to accept this as their personality and work from there. The personality of a person over the age of twenty will not easily be changed. However, if the symptoms are not severe, and if the tendency for dependency is only in a very limited part of their life, or if the person is still in their teens, then there are steps that can be taken. You must introduce this person to a totally new reality outside of their small world.

This kind of young person has a view of the world which is centered upon himself or herself. Because of that, they are unable to easily acknowledge other values.

In order to show how wide and full of possibilities the real world is, and in order to expose a person to a variety of value systems, you must deliberately change their actions and experiences. The simplest way is to have them set off on a trip during which they are responsible for themselves. This method has very good results. It is also effective to invite them into a totally different world through a new hobby.

If you see this tendency in yourself and it worries you, then I recommend that you try the same method on yourself. Expose yourself to new and unfamiliar experiences. Try going into a kind of shop you've never gone into before. Listen to a kind of music you have never heard before. Try a totally new food. Try changing what you wear. Through the repetition of these simple steps you will find that you are able to broaden your own world considerably.

Knowing exactly just what kind of person you really are is not an easy thing to do. Try broadening your horizons little by little and you will eventually find a place that is just right for you. If you continue this kind of simple effort, you will surely be able to come to know yourself better.

THE LIE THAT "PEOPLE CAN CHANGE"

Recently there has been an increase of patients appearing at my clinic with no real problem except a desire to "change themselves." It's clear to me that they lack confidence in themselves and suffer from a vague kind of uneasiness.

If I give them a battery of psychological and personality tests, they seem happy and satisfied. But, then they ask: "Okay, then what exactly can I do to change myself?" and I am at a loss. I know all too well that a person's personality does not change very easily at all.

We've all seen the old movies in which the distinguished-looking psychiatrist puts the patient under hypnosis and finds out that the cause of a problem is some trauma that occurred in his or her childhood. The patient, upon awakening, sheds tears of joy and proclaims himself to be "cured." Many of the patients who come to my clinic are hoping for this miraculous kind of scenario, but it rarely occurs.

It seems that the desire to change oneself is a very basic one. If this desire is not managed properly, you end up becoming what I call a "life shifter" or a kind of roaming nomad.

Akemi, for example, is a thirty-seven-year-old single woman. When she was twenty-four, she decided she wanted to do "more meaningful work" and quit her job as a high school teacher to go to Africa with the Japan Overseas Cooperation Volunteers (JOCV). When I asked her for more details about this, she admitted that truthfully, she just couldn't stand the atmosphere in the faculty room at school anymore. However, she failed the exam for the JOVC and in the end, took a job with an apparel maker. When she was sent as a dispatch worker to work in an established department store, sales increased so much that she advanced to the position of manager with six months. But again, she quit her job.

After that she became an aide in a hospital for patients, working the night shift. "This work really helps people, and since I have days off I can meet my boyfriend easily," she claimed. But in fact she was having an affair with a married man, the father of two children, whom she had met while at the department store. This was the real reason she quit that job.

When this relationship went sour, she took a job in yet another office. In the process of switching jobs so many times she finally came up against age limitations in hiring and was unable to find employment.[3] But she remained carefree, saying, "Perhaps I'll tap all the experiences I've had and become an actress or a writer."

Next is the case of Sachiko. Sachiko does not switch jobs, but instead switches men. When she

---

[3] Although "lifetime employment" is not as prevalent in Japan as before, it is still difficult for a woman to find new employment after she enters her thirties.

was a student her boyfriend was "quite handsome, but I finally realized he wasn't very smart." About an older classmate she got involved with she said, "He treated me well and was very sincere, but he's boring." About another classmate she said, "I thought he was very mature, but it turns out he is too selfish." She also got involved with a man she met while working part time. Even after she graduated and got a full time job, she fell in love with many different kinds of men, but broke up with them all saying, "No, he isn't the one. There has to be a man who will understand and be just right for me." Now she says she is dating a man who "has a beautiful aura" but who actually seems to have some element of danger to him.

THE PERSONALITY OF A LIFE SHIFTER

Both Akemi and Sachiko are creditable and excellent examples of life shifters. If you have ever heard yourself say, over and over, "There has to be a better job (man) out there for me" then you, too, may be a member of this troubled club.

A life shifter is a person who constantly jumps here and there in search of a better job or a better mate and is forever changing his or her circumstances to find it. Unable to remain very long in one place, they live precarious lives.

Life shifting itself is not a bad thing at all. By putting yourself into a variety of different circumstances, you can discover what you really need and what is really the most suitable situation for yourself. The process of life-shifting can also be considered "a journey of self-discovery" and is a necessary one during certain stages of life.

However, if you have reached your mid-thirties and are still life-shifting regularly in search of yourself, then things become more problematic. If you life-shift well and grow in the process, good for you, but if you are bringing yourself only to lower levels, then life-shifting is not as beneficial to you as it once was.

A life shifter is looking to the exterior world—a job or a lover—to find self-fulfillment. They travel endlessly in search of an environment that will make them happy, without having to change their inner life. Ultimately, it is unlikely that they will find contentment with any job or relationship.

It is characteristic of a life shifter to put the blame of any bad results on outside sources. "This company has no intention of letting women advance, anyway" one will say, and switch jobs again. "My husband doesn't understand me" says another, and files for divorce. Lamenting a lack of friends a man will say, "Nobody really understands me."

Life-shifters fail to think deeply. Even if they fail in their jobs, they often shrug it off saying, "No

point worrying about this forever." If they have unsuccessful relationships they say to themselves,
"Well, he just wasn't the right one" and start looking for a new boyfriend the next day. It may appear
as if they are positive thinkers, but this is not really
the case.

Actually, most life-shifters strike me as scared.
They are unable to take a good look at themselves
and discover where they have gone wrong. If they
were to confront themselves they would see that
they have made inconsistent actions in their lives,
and become confused. They might hate themselves
for living so far removed from their ideals. It turns
out that they are life shifting not to discover their
own needs, but to run away from their inner selves.

KNOWING YOUR TRUE SELF

The problem with life-shifters is that they travel
the paths of life holding a remote control switch.
When they find themselves in circumstances that
are unpleasant for them, they say, "this TV show is
boring" and change channels. With one click of the
button they change the scenery of their lives.

In doing this, life-shifters never reach the stage
of being able to see their true self. They don't have
any idea of what they really want to do. So what
happens? They become unable to express anything

but the most trivial desire that appears on the surface of their heart. Trivial needs that we have change with each passing day. In the end, they are led around by the nose by nothing but the stimulus before their them and end up living life for the moment only.

There are people who use life-shifting to improve their lives. There is nothing wrong with saying, "This is what I want to do, but the company that I am with now doesn't give me an opportunity in this area, so I'm going to find a new job." Here the motivation is clear. But the motivation of a life-shifter is vague. "I just really don't like this job." Or, "I want to do something more fulfilling."

A life-shifter does not make his move in order to utilize what he has reaped thus far in his career, but instead finds a totally new role for himself. He moves not vertically, but horizontally, so he is unable to achieve much personal depth in any field. Where is the end of the road?

If you think that you are one of those people in the "reserve troops" for life-shifting, try the following five steps. (If you are a person totally without doubts, or a "chronic accommodator," or if you are a person unable to find what you want to do in life, then these steps should be useful for you as well.)

1. Be aware of the hidden needs within yourself
A life-shifter is unable to see his real self and lives

in a world of daydreams. "How I am now is not the real me." "If I could just find the right job that taps the ability lying dormant inside of me, then I'd really come alive." Because their real selves are repugnant to them, life-shifters tend not to exist in the real world. They are unaware of their real needs. Their denial of their true feelings is what causes their frustration.

If you understand your own hidden needs, you can make good use of your career steps and relationships to avoid going in circles. In most cases a person's needs are simple things—wanting to be pampered or wanting to be the center of attention. If you have these needs, admit to them. Then you won't need to waste time taking the long way around.

2. Take responsibility for your actions

Stop taking the passive position of expecting happiness to come through more meaningful work or through a relationship with a person who truly understands you. Instead of saying, "I wonder if I will ever find a place to work that will really give me a chance," look to the future thinking, "I know what I want to do." Move forward purposefully; don't just drift.

If one of your life-shifts ends in a failure along the way, take the blame for it yourself. You made the choice for that shift and you must bear the responsibility for the results. Even if you fail at something, if you can look at yourself and how you have been affected by it, you will at least gain that insight. You can always grow from the experience.

3. Use the shift as a step on the way to finding yourself
What kind of work you do, and what kind of person you are romantically involved with are important things, but don't get too caught up with them. Both your work and your relationships are only means to helping you find yourself. Try to look at them as a kind of stage setting for a human drama in which you are the hero. You can't change yourself merely by changing the props. The only thing that can bring you happiness is yourself— no other person or thing has the ability to create your happiness.

4. Look for a situation that feels good
All of us have different aspects to our personality. There is a part of me that wishes to be adored and get a lot of attention, and there is a part of me that wants to be sharp and self-sufficient. You may have many different aspects of your personality, but it is important to be aware of which aspect of your personality feels the best to you. Even without changing jobs or relationships you can at least simulate situations or circumstances in your head and try to figure out what feels right.

Try telling yourself that you are not a life-shifter,

try not switching jobs for awhile, and try to be content. Act out being that person. You may be surprised to find that you have been denying yourself and overaccommodating to the world around you.

5. Try imagining a different life

If you have become aware of some hidden need recently, congratulations! You are on the way to seeing what it is that you really want out of life. Now, in order to realize those needs, start to consider in what way you should live your life. This time imagine yourself not as the self who has up until now been in many different situations, but instead try imagining yourself and your life as a whole.

DECEIVE YOURSELF TO BRING LUCK

Deceiving yourself is different from self-deception. When I talk about "deceiving yourself," I am not talking about tricking yourself, but more about using auto-suggestion to change your circumstances for the better.

Auto-suggestion has the power to regulate a person's actions without them being aware of it. If somebody says to you everyday, "You look really full of energy today" or "You look so healthy" then you actually begin to feel that energy. It is said that this even has the power to cure mild disorders. Conversely, if someone should repeatedly say to you, "Is something wrong?" or "You don't look well today" then you begin to feel unwell. Even though you are not actually sick or in bad condition it is possible for a psychogenic disorder to develop.

Auto-suggestion really does have an enormous amount of power over us.

The iron-clad rule for using auto-suggestion is that it must be done in a low-key manner. It must very casually steal into the very depths of the heart. Rather than being told firmly by one person that "you don't look well today" it is much more effective if a number of people occasionally say it to you. In that way it will lodge itself in your consciousness. (Those television commercials that air over and over again on any given day using the same jingles are doing it with just this expectation.)

As a doctor, this is not an action that I can recommend, but it is easy to cause a person to feel sick. If a few people get together and agree upon this action and say suggestively, "Aren't you feeling ill?" or something along those lines to some innocent victim, there are sure to be some results. If you say that to a middle aged person, usually there is some kind of physical condition that they can relate it to, causing them to actually become ill in a short period of time.

How does auto-suggestion work? Is it really posoible to remodel yourself for the better by using auto-suggestion?

If you really believe this deep within your heart then almost anything is possible through auto-suggestion. However, if deep down in your heart you really do not believe what you are telling yourself, then no matter how many times you say to yourself "I'll be company president" you can't expect it to work. It will always be an unfulfilled dream.

It might appear that people who lack total conviction will be unable to effectively use auto-suggestion. But that is not actually the case. Even those people who lack self-confidence will gradually come to have more confidence in themselves. And there is a phrase that can be used to change their destiny for the better: "Day-by-day, in every way, I am getting better and better."

This expression to use for auto-suggestion is the brilliant work of the French scholar Emile Coué. Coué recommends that these words be said to oneself twenty times before going to bed and another twenty times upon awaking in the morning. There is no need to use these exact words. What is important is to put the emphasis on "in every way," "day-by-day" and "getting better and better."

From a specialist's point of view, this kind of auto-suggestion is called a "general auto-suggestion." Some people may think that it is self-deception or a lie. But actually it is the real truth.

In order to have a specific auto-suggestion such as "I'm going to be company president" be effective, it is necessary for this kind of general auto-suggestion to be lurking at the bottom of one's consciousness. Because of this, I'd recommend first and foremost that you recite these words to yourself for a month.

When you try auto-suggestion, it is best to be in a relaxed state. Try it in the evening, after you have bathed and are in your pajamas. In the morning do it before you get out of bed and while taking deep breathes. This will enhance the effect. If you repeat it to yourself with the pure faith of a child (without doubting the results) in just one month you should be able to realize a positive shift in your feelings. As each day passes you will begin to see your life open more and more.

How about giving yourself a reward?

I have a good friend from my college days who loves to drink saki. All he has to do is hear the word "saki" and he becomes aroused by the image almost to the point of drooling. In our student days he would drink a *sho* (1.8 liters) of saki every day. It was enough to make me worry about his future!

He is over the age of forty now, but has yet to become an alcoholic. He is still a drinker, though. But when he reached the age of thirty, he stopped drinking every day. Even though he loved to drink saki, he made the decision that "I'll drink saki only three days a week." And he has stuck religiously to that plan. There is no indication at this time that he has any dependency problem with alcohol.

From my point of view, drinking three days a week seems like plenty. But to a saki-lover like him it is "anguish equal to torture." He says that on a hot summer's evening, just the thought of a cold beer going down is enough to make it impossible to concentrate on work. And in the winter, there is a different kind of agony at that thought of a nice warm cup of saki at dinner to take off the chill and warm one's stomach.

I finally told him that if he really liked to drink that much, he should cut down on the amount, but enjoy his saki everyday instead of just three times a week. But he answered with the following:

"When I start drinking, I want to drink a lot. If I can't drink until I am satisfied, then it isn't any fun for me. If I really get going I can drink all night. But if I did that all the time, then I'd have to quit my job. So, that is why I decided to just drink three days a week. On top of that, if I drink everyday it is just a bad habit. But if I can only drink every two days, then it is a kind of reward for myself. I drink as a reward for working as hard as I can at the office. Even if that is really a lie, if I believe it then I work hard and accomplish a lot at work. And the saki tastes even better going down. In fact, it tastes even better than it would if I was drinking it everyday."

Unless you love to drink like my friend does, it may be hard to understand this kind of reasoning. Through the regular practice of lying to himself, he is using saki as a stimulating force. He is able to keep away from a dependency relationship with liquor and instead use it to increase his zeal for work. This kind of theory would work for a person who held the belief that "saki=life." From a psychological standpoint, he is creating motivation for his success in life and work.

Motivation is at the root of human action. It is motivation that determines where and how long we will travel. When a child does not want to do his homework, the parent saying, "When you're done with that page, you can go outside and play" can cause an unexpected show of enthusiasm towards the assignment. This, too, is motivation, in the form of a reward.

Human beings are not prone to making great effort unless there exists some kind of motivation. With the right motivation, even a person lacking in perseverance will be able to make some efforts. If you train yourself well with motivation, you will even be able to complete a disagreeable task quickly, so long as some small reward lies at the end of it.

Even if my previous example of my friend the drinker doesn't convince all of my readers, think about creating motivation in your own life. When you have a long and disagreeable task in front of you, it is a good idea to set up some kind of reward for yourself such as "when I finish this work, I'm going to take off an extra day on the weekend and take a trip with my wife somewhere."

ALL WORDS HAVE LIES IN THEM

Up until this point, I have separated truth from lies.

But when you look deeply into the essence of a lie, you begin to see that the borderline between the truth and a lie is very fuzzy. Just as there are many different levels of a lie, there are also different levels of the truth. To me, the truth and lies are like an onion, with thin layers of truth interspersed with layers of lies. It is very complex.

For example, often a child will cry to his parents, "Buy me this toy!" Whether these words actually represent the child's true feelings is hard to judge. It may be that the child does not actually want the toy, but instead is looking for love from his parents. Or, he wants his parents to say to him, "You're much too old for a toy like that. Choose a different one." In this case he is actually looking for his parents to acknowledge his growth. Of course it may be that he really *does* want the toy that badly. It is difficult to know what meaning really lies behind the surface of the words.

This is not just applicable to children. If your girlfriend were to say to you, "I never want to see your face again" it may be that she is just saying this in a fit of anger and her real feelings are the exact opposite. These kinds of reverse statements can often be seen in the world of business, and indeed occur in many situations in everyday life.

In addition to the surface meaning of words, words may be wrapped in several meanings. In most of these cases, the real meaning hidden beneath is, in context to the surface meaning, a lie. What kind of hidden lies occur the most? Of course there are no accurate statistics for this kind of thing, but from my own experience, it seems like most of these cases involve the expression of our own emotions and feelings.

Emotions such as being happy or sad or jealous have a very strong feel to them. However, those exact feelings are difficult to express accurately with words. The moment we put these feelings into words, the words themselves take on a meaning of their own, differing from the original feeling.

THROUGH DECEPTION, YOU CAN CHEER SOMEBODY UP

All of us at some time in our life find ourselves in a state of inertia. There are many ways to solve this problem. You can go out and get drunk and forget about it. You can immerse yourself in a new hobby. Or you can tell yourself that "life isn't always perfect" and simply accept this state as a normal, occasional occurrence. Everyone has their own way of dealing with this state.

When feeling inertia, it is often very effective to physically exert yourself. Taking a trip to a new place and exposing yourself to fresh experiences is also a good method. However there is another method that gives consistently good results.

Among salespeople, who are always under great pressure to meet their quotas, there are many who have the knack for keeping their spirits up even when things are down. A certain salesman in a medium-sized company told me that when he has fallen behind in sales and is having trouble meeting his quota, he always pays a visit to a prosperous shop. It doesn't matter what kind of shop it is. A restaurant, a coffee shop or a bookstore—as long as it is a store crowded with people from off the street, it makes no difference.

Just going into the shop alone does not cause his spirits to rise. He looks around and observes. There is always something that impresses him, whether it is the level of customer service, good food, or unusual sales items with high appeal.

When he is able to figure out quickly what the reason for the shop's success is, he says he stops worrying. He begins to see the way out of his slump. After that, he puts a little more power into his voice than usual when he makes his pitch, and soon he is back to his old, confident self.

Human moods can be revived through very small changes in our routine. Before you begin your work day, decide on your own special "jinx." When you go to work, try taking a different route than you usually do. Through just these small stimuli it is possible to raise your own consciousness. I recommend you all find a method of stirring things up and tricking yourself so that you, too, can keep your spirits up.

Chapter 3
LIES TO MAKE
A WOMAN MORE
BEAUTIFUL

LIES THAT WOMEN TELL ARE JUST STOPGAPS

In general, women tell lies to protect themselves and are without any underlying malicious intent. You could even say that women's lies are often more innocent and charming when compared to men's lies. Of course, there may be men who disagree, saying, "But you should see what my girlfriend pulled on me!" But in most of those cases, it is unlikely that women will start out thinking, "I'm going to really trick him."

Women as a rule do not tell premeditated lies, but instead lie on the spur of the moment to cover a particular situation. Eventually that lie will come back to haunt her or necessitate a bigger lie. And, eventually those lies are more often than not discovered.

Actually there are few really evil women, such as the one portrayed by Sharon Stone in the popular movie "Basic Instinct," a woman who gets away with the perfect lie over many years. But her lie really was a perfect lie. It was based on her knowledge of how the person involved would think and act. Because her lie seemed to be almost too outrageous, the other character believed that it was true. She was not telling a lie to protect herself, but in order to continue murdering people. In fact, it could be said that she was enjoying her lies.

Strangely enough, even though her role was that of an "evil heroine," that character gained the audience's favor. Usually, the "bad guy" ends up destroying him or herself, but in her case, it ended with her getting away tricking everyone around her. Believe it or not, there are many men who wish they could meet an evil woman like Sharon Stone!

By contrast, the average woman's lie is an innocuous one. Women lie so that people will think better of them. Or, they lie to get a man's attention, or to look good in front of their peers or other women. These lies are a little pathetic. If you are going to tell a lie in the first place, don't stop at such a trivial one, but instead tell a really big one. Tell a lie that will be big enough to help you get ahead in your workplace or one that will catch a man for you.

In order to do that, you must have enough confidence to be able to look a person straight in the eye with the attitude of "So what?" if the lie is discovered. Whether or not you have confidence in yourself is the testing point for determining whether or not you can get away with telling a lie.

LIES THAT ARE OKAY TO TELL

We Japanese have an expression that says, "A lie is sometimes expedient." Unlike the Americans, whose ancestors were strict Puritans, we Japanese have a culture which accepts the use of a lie to lubricate certain situations in society. When doing business, "I'll think about it" has the same meaning as saying no, but it is a softer way of declining. However, this kind of culture has been difficult for Westerners to understand.

It's unpleasant to find yourself having to tell a passive lie just to protect yourself. Ironically, you may find yourself in a worse position than before. If you are going to constantly be worrying over whether you will be caught telling a lie, then it is better not to lie in the first place.

There is the case of Ms. Saito, who lived an elite, upper-class life in Europe and was the author of a book on positive thinking, entitled *Super First-Class*. When it was discovered that her whole blue-blooded background was actually made up, it caused quite a scandal. But I understand that many of her readers continued to support her, saying, "It doesn't matter that her background is made up, because her life itself is so interesting." Her seminars on positive thinking remain just as popular as before she was "exposed." If you can tell a lie skillfully and blatantly enough, it can become the truth. It is easiest to fool people with a very bold lie. If you are going to tell a lie, let Ms. Saito be your guide.

Another good lie is one done for the benefit of another person. If you are invited to dinner by a man that you have no interest in, you can refuse saying, "I'm sorry, but I already have plans for today." This kind of lie helps to keep relationships between people smooth. There are people who worry about telling this kind of trivial lie, but it seems clear to me that lying is the best recourse in this case for everyone concerned.

Contrary to what most of us believe, the person who is *unable* to tell a lie is not a very caring person. In fact, most of these people are often lacking in consideration of others and have no warmth. They are finicky, self-centered people who often hurt others.

Lies told by women that help smooth the paths of life are a positive thing. But it is important that they be told skillfully. An obvious lie that will soon be discovered will only have the effect of inflicting a greater hurt upon the person concerned.

LIES TO MAKE YOURSELF MORE BEAUTIFUL

Women today are under a lot of pressure to meet certain standards of society. The influence of Western culture today calls for shapely legs, though in Japan this part of the body was traditionally hidden by a kimono. The art of make-up is now truly an art. Exercising has become popular and spas are on the rise everywhere.

In the past, the difference between a beautiful woman and an ugly one was well defined. But these days, with a little bit of effort and creativity, women can transform themselves so that the borderline becomes unclear. The women I see walking down the street are nearly all pretty. Even if one is not born a beauty, one can diet, wear the latest fashions, apply make-up and take care of herself. There are even corrective undergarments for sale now, so that any woman can have a glamorous figure. It could be said that this is a kind of wonderful lie only allowed to women.

Having said that, it can also be said that many of these women start to look the same. Westerners comment that it is hard to tell one long-haired fashionable Japanese woman from another. First and foremost, fashion exists so that a woman can look more beautiful than everyone else. But recently it seems to be more for the purpose of looking *the same* as everyone else. Many women, in my opinion, are sacrificing their individuality for looks.

It is a strange thing, but a beautiful woman with a symmetrically perfect face is actually less striking than that of a woman with a slight imperfection to her. If you leaf through a magazine, this becomes obvious. A model who just a few years ago might be on the borderline of being called ugly is now featured in many photos and labeled "a unique beauty."

Even in Japan's entertainment world, it seems that a unique and individual beauty is now more popular than a more typical beauty. A woman with a perfectly symmetrical face with well-formed features is beautiful upon first glance, but after time can seem artificial. A perfect beauty has ceased to be a beauty. These days a woman who has a certain oddness to her is the one that will be considered the "real" beauty.

If this is the case, then anything goes. If the mass media declares a certain woman to be beautiful, then from that day she reigns. If somebody's popularity is on the rise, then magazines quickly put together feature stories on her, claiming that "she is this year's new look." They bombard us with claims that this year short hair will be "in." Just when the streets of the city are filled with women with short hair cuts, they suddenly announce that now long hair is "in." A woman would need to be able to grow her hair back overnight to keep up!

BELIEVE YOU ARE BEAUTIFUL

Stop letting the mass media mislead you. And stop conforming to society's idea of beauty; women are beautiful unto themselves. Try to make the most of your own individuality when you make your fashion statement.

Still, you may be thinking to yourself that your nose is too flat, or your legs are too thick. A women's heart is always bothered by the flaws she perceives. There is probably not a single woman who would admit to being one hundred percent satisfied with her face or proportions. But we have all seen an alluring women who seems to sparkle in a special way. On careful inspection you can see that she may not really be as beautiful as she seems, but she has that special something that makes her appear very pretty. What is that special quality?

The answer is simple. It is because she doesn't waste time worrying about her flaws or getting overly concerned about small things. It is not that she is unaware of her faults, or that she has resigned herself to them. In fact, just the opposite. She is well aware of her flaws, but she is able to camouflage them and make them work for her.

Being aware of your flaws or weak points is the first step towards becoming more beautiful. Knowing your own imperfections and exactly why they are imperfections gets you halfway to the goal of transforming yourself into a more beautiful woman. In fact, you can even change your flaws into advantages. If your mouth is too large, then use bright red lipstick instead of trying to cover it up. Be bold about it—make it work for you.

A woman can make dramatic changes in her image with a new hairstyle, make-up or clothes. The worst thing a woman can do is to just sit and worry about her looks without trying anything. When a woman stops caring about her hair and make-up, even the expression on her face becomes gloomy. What a waste to make yourself ugly!

First start with the wish to become more beautiful. Every morning look into the mirror and tell yourself, "I am getting prettier every day. I am a unique beauty." Chant it to yourself like a mantra. Even if you have some doubts and are wondering what good telling that kind of lie will do, keep repeating it to yourself everyday. Over time, even a little lie like this can really make you feel more beautiful.

This is the truth: the more unique your face is, the more beautiful you become. Being beautiful in the same way as others won't really make you beautiful at all. Incorporate your own uniqueness into your hair style and clothes.

In Europe, a fashionable woman may be a fan of Hermes or Yves St. Laurent, but she also has clothes designed specifically for herself at some of the finest shops that do not have any designer attached to them. To wear the same brand of clothes as everyone else is considered by such women to be passé and in bad taste. It is better to ignore what you see in magazines and find what is right for you personally.

One member of a personnel department at a big company said, "If I tell a woman that she is 'different' she seems very happy. Even though I did not have the intention of praising her, these days being 'different' seems to be considered a compliment." Yes, no matter what anyone else says, you are beautiful. Just as if you keep telling a lie it can become the truth, you can also become more beautiful if you believe that you are beautiful. Strangely enough those around you will also begin to believe.

LIES TO CAPTURE A MAN'S HEART

In all ages and in all countries an enigmatic woman shrouded in mystery draws attention from those around her. Falling in love starts with the feeling that "I want to know more about this woman." However, no matter how much interest you have in a person, the longer that you are involved in a relationship, the less there is to discover. It begins to get old. When the two of you reach the point where you are so comfortable with each other that there are no more surprises, then the man starts to stop seeing you as a woman. A woman should not ever fully open up to a man nor let him know her completely, but should always have a certain unknown part to her. This is the key to making love last.

A certain woman told her boyfriend, "After three years, I will tell you my secret." The boyfriend tried very hard to get her to reveal her secret, but she remained adamant that she would tell him only after three years. Two years passed. At that point, he remembered what she had said, and said to her, "In just one more year you're going to tell me that secret, right?" She replied to him, "There is no secret. I just said that to you to make sure that you would be with me for three years."

Rather than getting angry with her, he thought it was very charming and their relationship continued. She had succeeded in skillfully manipulating her man's heart.

When you look at the results of questionnaires in women's magazines entitled "Why I fell for her" or "What made me fall back in love with her," one of the top-ranking reasons is "I discovered something new and unexpected about her." Finding out that a woman who appeared very serious and uptight really liked to dance the night away at discos, or that a woman who appeared to care only about her looks really liked to read high-level literature, added a new element to the relationship.

Here is another example. One man told me recently, "I was going out with this very cute girl who wore her hair in curls and always had frilly clothes. I got bored with her, stopped seeing her as often, and started to avoid her. She told me that she wanted to know exactly what was or wasn't happening with us. That gave me the opportunity I had been looking for and when we next met I was planning to break it off with her. But when she walked in the door, she was wearing jeans, no make-up and was even puffing on a cigarette. When I expressed my surprise, she said, "Well, this is the real me. I was just trying to be fashionable before. But since there is no more reason to try and impress you and dress for you, well...."

He was so surprised that he wondered how he had missed seeing her true personality and said, "I'm breaking up with the old you, but now I want to start anew with the real you!"

Now you may say this particluar man seems like a bit of a simpleton, but it does seem that if you let a man discover a part of you that has remained hidden so far, he will be drawn to you. However, for a woman to keep a part of her hidden requires a lot of effort.

Some good ways to discover a new you are to try reading a book from a completely different genre than you're used to, or to listen to a different kind of music. You may even surprise yourself and discover new aspects of yourself you didn't realize you had. Real love does not come from just being flattered by a man. Even when you are away from him, you should constantly strive to improve yourself. Sometimes it doesn't hurt to turn him down, saying something like, "I can't get together today. I've gotten really into fishing and I'm too busy." Just be careful: a man won't keep chasing after you endlessly. But sometimes by making yourself unavailable, you can make him think, "Hmmm, she has something in her life that is more important to her than me." Keeping him a little on the edge this way is an important thing.

Jealousy is the potion that activates love. It can be very effective in turning the tables around when you need to. It isn't necessary to reveal everything to a man right away. It's good to have a part of yourself that is unavailable to him. Being mysterious isn't really so much a technique, but a belief that it isn't necessary to tell everything. For example, you say, "I went out to a nice restaurant the other day" and he asks, "With whom?" and you answer, "Just with a friend." Say no more than that. Instead of always pushing or insisting, try backing off sometimes. Even though he trusts you absolutely, when you are deliberately vague like this it will cause him to be a little on guard.

Don't always throw a straightball, but vary your pitches with a few curves. These kind of tactics increase love and are the secret to closing the distance between the two of you. And remember that just because you do everything for a man does not mean that he will always love you. Doing everything for a man is like traveling on a one-way street that will not become any wider; love will not deepen from that. You must work to get him involved in you or else the love between you will not grow.

LIES THAT MEN WHO "REALLY CARE" TELL

Running away, betrayal, irresponsibility, lying. There are many women who have had their hearts broken by the actions of men. Even though there can be no guarantees in love, these are things most people don't want to experience.

"I was doing it for you" is what they often say when exposed, but a certain amount of cunningness is hidden in this kind of speech and behavior. For example, these words can make you think, "This guy really cares." But in reality he is just indecisive. When women list the qualities that make up their ideal man, the top one is always, "a caring man," but be careful when you find a man like this. You may end up paying a price.

Recently it appears that caring and attentive men who are willing to give their all for a woman have increased in number. "He comes to pick me up the minute I call," I have women say, or "He never forgets to give me a present on Christmas and my birthday." These kind of "caring guys" are actually cleverly using women.

Men, who when they were younger were never objects of love, but often used by women and thought of as friends, strangely enough suddenly become the ideal mate when women are ready to settle down. "I thought he was too sweet and caring, and not very exciting as a boyfriend, but when it comes to marriage, that type is good," I often hear. "I will be happy if I find a man who loves me and is willing to do anything for me." However, I've noticed that many women who have married this kind of caring man and should be very happy, turn up at my clinic in a state of depression.

The following is an actual true case of mine.

Reiko is a young, active woman who is very beautiful and was quite popular in her youth. She fell in love quite a few times and enjoyed a long period of being single. At 35 she fell in love for the last time and got married. Her husband was a 40-year-old computer specialist. They met at a temple where both of them were practicing zazen meditation as a hobby, and they were married six months later. Since both of them had been single for a long time, they had many hobbies and interests and agreed "we are both adults who have a lot of different experiences, so we will respect each other's sep-arate lives." With this thought they committed to marriage.

After not even half a year of married life, Reiko began to suffer from insomnia and anxiety and came to the clinic for a check-up. When I listened to her speak I could see signs of depression. Al-though she repeated over and over that her hus-band "really cared about her" those words seemed to point to something important.

Her husband had said to her, "You don't need to cook for me. I want you to be able to do what you want to do." Most women would be very envious of such a situation. If Reiko went out drinking with her friends or returned home to her parents for long periods, he didn't say a word. Whether she spent one night away, or three or four, he only said, "If you are happy then I'm happy" or "It makes me happy to see you enjoying yourself." He never com-plained at all.

When Reiko began to feel depressed, he became even more caring and would drive her to and from the clinic. If she failed to prepare any meals, do the laundry or cleaning and merely stayed in bed all day, he would take over and do it all. Since he had been a bachelor for many years he was able to han-dle all the household chores easily. However, the more caring he became the worse Reiko's depres-sion got. Eventually, Reiko said that she felt more comfortable being at a friend's house and began staying there regularly. Even though she was gone for over a week her husband merely said, "If that will help you get better...." and was willing to wait.

Reiko's depression was obviously rooted in her husband's actions. What she really wanted was to be useful and needed. Her husband was the type who could live easily on his own. A marriage should be because two people want and need each other. If this is not the case, then there is little meaning to sharing a life. In Reiko's case, the two had gotten married but were actually continuing their own respective single lives under the same roof.

A statement such as "if it makes you happy it is fine with me" seems to be one of understanding and caring, but it really is not; it is a kind of escape. What they are really saying is, "Figure out what you need to be happy by yourself. It isn't my responsibility." The truly caring man would say something like, "I want you to be very happy, so I want you to make me happy as well."

A wife whose husband has little to say about anything, who respects the fact that they have their own separate lives, and who doesn't seem to mind whether she is around or not, will feel much emptiness in her life. It is natural that she become depressed. The fact that she has such an understanding husband puts her in the position of being unable to complain. "He is so understanding with me," she thinks. "What is wrong with me?" She ends up blaming herself, creating a vicious cycle.

What Reiko really wanted was for her husband to say to her, "I can't live without you." Many of the wives in the world who have less-than-perfect husbands and complain "He can't do a thing for himself" are actually pretty happy and content. All of them are thinking, "without me he'd be lost."

When I told Reiko's husband the real cause of her depression, he was very surprised. The next day he went right over to the friend's house where she had been staying and clearly told her, "I want you to come home!"

I'd like to say that after that the two of them lived happily ever after, but people's personalities do not change that easily. This husband continued to be a man of few needs from his wife and Reiko's insomnia did not get better.

When you go on a date with your boyfriend, does he often say, "I don't care where we go, it's up to you?" That may not be out of flexibility or catering to your needs. It may be because he doesn't want to take the trouble of deciding. If you marry this kind of man, and when you someday need to make decisions about finances or your children, he may also say, "I don't care. It's up to you." Whether it is just for a date or for life, you should choose a person who will talk things over with you and decide things together.

You may be attracted to a man who stands in front of your house waiting until you come home, or a man who sees you home even though his own home may be an hour away in the opposite direction, or a man who takes the day off on your birthday, etc. This kind of man who seems to be almost overly attentive and caring will not last too long unless he has an awful lot of free time. And you can also be sure that such a man will not have a successful career at work.

If it was just that, it might still be okay, but if you marry a man with few hobbies or interests of his own he'll end up sitting around the house doing nothing on his days off like a big piece of *sodaigomi*[4].

So think about it. Is the man in your life really a "caring" one?

LIES IN THE BEDROOM

Although you really love him, you find yourself unsatisfied in bed. On top of that, he, unfortunately,

---

[4] sodai gomi literally means "large-sized garbage." Traditionally in Japan, there is one day a month when large unneeded items may be put out for curbside collection. More recently the term has been used by women to represent retired men at home. Having spent their whole lives devoted to work, they are unable to amuse themselves and their presence at home is quite bothersome to their wives.

believes himself to be a great lover. If you were to express your dissatisfaction directly, he would surely be very hurt.

And if you were to start giving him orders about what you wanted him to do in bed, then he might wonder about your past. "If he would only touch me somewhere else," you think in frustration as you pretend to be having orgasm after orgasm. Your lover gains more and more confidence in his technique as a lover and you become more and more frustrated and unable to tell him the truth.

I know from my practice that there are an unexpectedly large number of women who don't express their true desires in bed. It is not unusual to find women who have kept up this charade for years and never once experienced orgasm. Many women give up and quickly fake an orgasm, thinking that if they aren't going to feel anything, they just want to get it over with as fast as possible. The men, on the other hand, believe that "the way to tell if a woman really has an orgasm is whether or not she is sweating" or some such nonsense. Although women these days are more aggressive than ever, they are still unable to assert themselves fully in the bedroom.

According to specialists, your sexual style often becomes set in your twenties. You believe that "this way is the best way for me." This tendency is particularly strong in men. The majority of men have no fundamental understanding at all of a woman's sexuality. In spite of that, after they have had sexual encounters with a few women, they claim to "understand a woman's body." Men's magazines often carry special features on "How to please a woman in bed." These articles also contribute to a man's belief that he knows everything he needs to know.

Our society continues to be one of double standards, and the myth that "a woman who is good in bed is a slut" still holds many believers, making women reluctant to take any leadership in bed. But in the last few years, there has been a slight change in things from the women's perspective. Sex manuals for women—written by women—have been quietly gaining in popularity. Books with the shocking message that "most women are faking it" have become best sellers. Books with such titles as *Joanna's Way to Love* or *Nora's Way to Make Love and Be Made Love To* share information on how two people can please each other the most in bed. It seems that women's sexuality is an issue in both Eastern and Western cultures.

The "sexual revolution" for women has certainly arrived. Women are fed up with sex that only pleases a man and want their share as well. I recommend that men stop relying on adult videos and men's magazines, and instead pick up one of the aforementioned books to read.

THE ART OF LYING

From reading these books the one thing that I can say is that sex for a woman must be an extension of "*skinship*."[5] Sex that does not include tender kisses and embraces, but instead is merely focused on the act itself, will not succeed in pleasing a woman. Many men believe that "if I put a lot of energy into it she'll be satisfied" but this is a big mistake. It is impossible for a woman to have any expectation of a man who lacks a light touch in bed.

Now let's look at some of the most pervasive lies that women tell themselves, to their own detriment.

LIE #1: BEING THIN WILL MAKE YOU HAPPY

More and more people all over the world are dieting—there seems to be no stopping the fitness boom. When women's magazine sales start to lag they put together a "diet issue" to increase sales. There is the "yogurt diet," "plantain diet," and the currently popular "salted diet." I'm amazed at the

---

[5] "Skinship" is a word that has been coined by the Japanese based on the English words friendship, kinship, etc. It is often used to describe the relationship between a mother and child. A mother whose relationship with her child seems distant could be said to be lacking in "skinship." Many Japanese believe this word to also exist in the English language.

kind of diets that they come up with. The very fact that new kinds of diets are constantly being invented suggests that none of them are very successful! But women never get tired of trying a new diet, and if you get any three women together you can be sure that the topic of conversation will turn to dieting. "If I could just lose 5 kilos" or "If my waist was just 3 centimeters smaller...." Almost all women have had these thoughts.

In commercials for diet foods and esthétiques, advertisers cleverly exploit this psychological state of women. "I lost 10 kilos in just three short months," "He finally fell in love with me," "Losing weight changed my life," or "I got the perfect job." These commercials give the false illusion that if you go on a diet, you can easily find happiness.

In the real world, losing weight alone will not be enough to get you a job or a boyfriend. Most women know this, but continue to blame any failure on their own appearance. When a woman is overweight her outlook on life tends to be very pessimistic. If her friends invite her to the beach she says, "I'm too fat to go." But if she loses weight, she believes her life will change and a more cheerful personality will appear. But life doesn't just become rosy all of a sudden.

People lacking in self-confidence are easily caught up in dieting. Some even become ill with such food disorders as anorexia and bulimia every time they try to diet. Strangely enough, many of my patients with anorexia and bulimia are actually very attractive—they really have no need to diet at all. What has made them feel that they need to be thinner?

The answer is simple. Since their childhood, they have grown up listening to remarks such as "You're so cute" and "What a pretty little girl!" This kind of woman is only able to feel valued when she looks pretty. Even though she has reaped the rewards of being beautiful, she feels frightened that she will lose her looks. As she passes through adolescence her body changes, and she naturally gains weight. She begins to feel ugly and is unable to accept the changes in her body. Even if she loses weight, she is unable to believe that she is thin enough and continues with drastic dieting. As this progresses, dieting itself becomes her reason for living.

In contrast, women who were not born particularly attractive rarely end up with eating disorders from dieting. This is because most of them, as they grew up, found different ways to gain approval from those around them, either through success in sports, academics, or some kind of interest. This is also the reason why men, who have been raised with the belief that "it is what's inside that counts, not a man's appearance" are rarely affected by eating disorders.

Treatment for women with chronic eating disorders is extremely complicated. Even though they may appear to be cooperative and ask, "How can I gain back some weight?" they are really subconsciously thinking "I don't want to get any fatter than this." They naturally choose low-calorie foods when they do eat and eat only small amounts. Then there are bulimic patients who do eat a lot but later vomit what they eat. They are even more difficult to treat, because vomiting has become a way to maintain control. "I feel uncomfortable when I can feel food in my stomach," they say. Their bodies are always in a state of starvation so they are often under attack by uncontrollable appetites. After they eat as much as they possibly can they feel sick with themselves and then vomit. When this is repeated their stomachs expand, and if they don't eat large amounts they cannot be satisfied. In the worst cases, there is danger of stomach rupture.

Even being hospitalized does these patients little good. This is because they all actually think that "I want to stay just as thin as I am now." When a target weight is determined, they accept it temporarily and eat, but after they check out of the hospital they set off quickly to the supermarket, go on a binge and then vomit. In severe cases they have been known to put rocks in their pockets when being weighed.

These women are always focused on eating. At some point they are not "eating to stay alive" but rather "staying alive to eat." They are slaves to their appetites. They probably had some idea of what they wanted to do after they dieted and became attractive, but the diet itself has now become the goal. No man is going to want a woman who weighs only eighty pounds. Sports and normal physical activites are also out of the question. Nobody would ever call such a woman beautiful, even as flattery.

If you are thinking that you would like to diet successfully, then begin right now. But there is no need to be thin other than to be in fashion. To live your life just to be thin is a waste of time. Remember, if you are unhappy the principal reason is never due to your being overweight.

LIE #2: MARRIAGE WILL BRING YOU HAPPINESS

When things are not going well at work, or when eating alone starts to become depressing, women's thoughts turn towards marriage. Even if that isn't the case, when they reach their mid-twenties, their parents and coworkers begin to ask them when they are going to settle down. In the tough job market today it may actually be easier to find a man to marry than to find a good job. I hear that there are

women college students who are putting more effort into *omiai* than job hunting.

However, it is unlikely that a marriage for escape
like this will turn out very well. Being married also
has its disagreeable aspects. In place of a horrible
boss you may now have to deal with a horrible
mother-in-law. Unless you have a firm belief that
the two of you are going to work hard and make a
happy life together your marriage will not continue
for any length of time.

At the clinic I see many cases of supposedly hap-
pily-married wives who are psychologically imbal-
anced and suffering from depression. Those who
had worked at their jobs enthusiastically before being married seemed to be most affected by feelings
of emptiness.

Kazumi, age thirty, is one of those types. She
passed her student days in the atmosphere of the
women's movement. She enjoyed her studies and
got good grades. But when she started to work at a
company she was suddenly faced with the reality of
discrimination. Men in the company who had been
hired at the same time were given important work
to do while she was merely assigned to do miscella-
neous tasks. When she finally got fed up with the
same monotonous work day after day somebody
came to her with a proposed *omiai*. She ended up
marrying the man. She had also become tired of lis-

tening to her family and coworkers ask her, "When are you going to get married?"

Soon after her marriage Kazumi became pregnant and quit her job. She was home every day alone with her baby. Since the baby was born very small she was unable to get out much. She couldn't enjoy her favorite pastime of shopping, or go out and meet her friends for a meal. She felt fortunate not to have to share a house with her mother-in-law, but it was also inconvenient not to have her around to help her with the baby. She couldn't relate well with the other wives in her neighborhood, who only wanted to talk about their husbands and children.

As time passed, Kazumi became exhausted with caring for the baby and was unable to sleep at night. Her husband had just reached a point in his career where things were beginning to get interesting. He was very busy at work, and came home later and later. She had no one to keep her company in the evening and found herself sitting aimlessly in front of the television waiting for her husband to come home. She felt empty inside. What was the meaning of her life up until now? Why had she studied so hard and for what end? As she began to wonder about these things, she began to feel bitterness towards her child: "If I hadn't had this baby, I'd be free to do what I wanted." Then she felt unable to forgive herself for having such thoughts. She began to blame herself and became even more depressed, believing that "I am a worthless mother."

When Kazumi appeared at my clinic holding her baby, she had started to drink heavily to help her fall asleep at night. She began to cry, saying, "I'm not fit to be a mother."

"When I see women all dressed up in a suit going off to work I become so envious I just can't stand it. They all have somewhere to go and I have nothing. It is hard to believe that when I was working there were days that it was so awful that I didn't even want to go into work. Now I feel like I'm not even part of society anymore. I want to go back to work so badly that I don't even care what kind of work I do."

"Since I have been married I have been lonelier than I've ever been in my life. The loneliness that I felt when I was on my own before getting married was nothing compared to this. The loneliness that I feel now will continue my whole life and there is no way out of it. I've lost my confidence to continue my life with my husband and child."

"My husband says that when the baby is a little bigger he doesn't mind if I find a part-time job, but I don't think that will help. Before I was married, I thought that marriage would give me a reason for living, but I was wrong. Now I regret that I didn't spend more time with myself, becoming more independent, before I settled down to marriage."

Although Kazumi had tried to escape from work, she now wanted to escape from family. But she had the responsibility of her baby and it was difficult to escape. She repeated over and over that looking at marriage as just another career change had been a big mistake.

REAL LOVE IS NOT BORN OUT OF DEPENDENCY

It has been said that getting a divorce takes about 100 times the energy that getting married took. This is especially true for a woman who has always been a housewife and has no salary of her own. She becomes very worried about how her life will be after the divorce. Because of this, there are many wives who feel some dissatisfaction with their husbands, but choose to endure those feelings rather than go through the anguish and expense of a divorce. Needless to say, this leads to a poor mental state. In severe cases, it can lead to memory loss. When a human being feels cornered with no way out, they bury their feelings in their heart, and try to escape from their present situation. It is a kind of self-defense mechanism.

One woman whose condition failed to improve no matter what medication was tried had her symptoms immediately disappear right after her divorce. When she appeared at the clinic her face was joyful and she looked like a new person. It was enough to make you wonder just exactly what marriage is. Wives understand this and often say, "I think if I get a divorce, I will feel better."

In the previous example of Kazumi, it was not so much that she had a problem with her husband, but that she had a problem with her role as mother and wife. She did not feel any resentment towards her husband. It could even be said that the fact that she had no real reason to want a divorce was contributing to her symptoms. She had no one else to blame, and so ended up hating herself.

In the end, Kazumi went back to work after putting her child into a day-care center. She feels guilt about that at times, but she seems to be fairly content now. She has once again begun to care about how she looks.

Many women do dream of having a man to depend on who will take care of them. They long to get married, quit their jobs, and let a man take responsibility for them. This may be fitting for a woman who wants to abandon her individuality, but this lifestyle will never be satisfying for those women who want to work and gain some acknowledgment for themselves in society.

Whether it is a relationship between a couple, parent and child, or friends, a relationship that is an equal partnership between two individuals is a good relationship. When one of the parties concerned is completely dependent upon the other, then that relationship will not be a fruitful one. True love will not come from such a union. As Kazumi said, "I feel happier now then when I was trying to be a good mother and a good wife."

Currently it is said that one out of every two couples will divorce. Obviously, the maxim that "Once you are married you are set for life" no longer holds true. It is far better to think hard and create a working life plan for yourself. There are many wives who complain of loneliness after being married that is far worse than the loneliness they suffered before marriage.

In the end, you will be alone some time in your life, and a person who cannot be happy alone will not be happy in a marriage. The time will come when your children will leave the nest and most likely you will be predeceased by your husband. So it makes sense now to learn to enjoy time spent by yourself.

Chapter 4
LIES TO HELP A MAN SUCCEED

MEN LIKE TO LOOK IMPORTANT

Women aren't the only ones who tell lies. Next, let's take a look at some of the lies that men often tell. I interviewed a few businessmen to find out what kind of lies they favor. Combined with the kinds of lies that women tell, it is clear that they cover every trick in the book.

Lies for showing off and looking more important
"I'm really tight with that guy at Such-and-Such Company," or "The reason I'm still stuck being section chief is because the general manager here hates me," or "My boss trusts me totally, so anything I say goes..."

More often than not, these kinds of lies are told to people in a position below oneself. Most of the people who tell lies like these are dissatisfied with

THE ART OF LYING

their present positions. They are actually thinking
that, "I should really be...." and then want to brag a
little to workers who are below them. This kind of
lie is the result of an inferiority complex turned inside out. Wanting to brag for no particular reason is
also indicative of a complex of needing approval
from those around you.

Lies told to women
"I might not look it, but I'm pretty high up there at
work," or "All of the executive leaders at my company are idiots (because this man has gotten no
recognition from them)" or "I love you more than
anyone else ever could..."

When men tell these lies to women in order to
make themselves look more important, they are
desperately seeking approval. It is the male equiv-
alent to women wanting approval for being beautiful and a good homemaker. What is interesting is
that men will rarely tell this kind of lie to their
wives or steady girlfriends. And, it is rare to see a
case in which a man gets competitive about his
girlfriend's appearance, or lies about how his girlfriend looks.

Both men and women usually like to make
themselves look good. But, most of them can do
this in harmless ways. It can even be said that these
lies are not really deliberate lies, but fill a role of
providing some relief from stress.

Women like to show themselves and be loved as being very beautiful and desirable. Men like to show themselves and be loved as being a man of importance. It is no exaggeration to say that the intertwining of these two theses accounts for the success of the human drama of love and marriage.

MEN WHO CAN'T TELL A CREDITABLE LIE

Recently, the number of men I see who have "mother complexes" seem to be increasing.

A "mother complex" is not really an official psychiatric term. It is a term that is often used loosely by the mass media to describe a man who is overly dependent on his mother and fails to strike out on his own.

Among such men are those who do need treatment and have some kind of psychological damage, as well as those who just enjoy being wrapped up in their mother's love. Without going into all the nuances, let's look at what most of us recognize as a "mother complex."

I entitled this section "Men who can't tell a creditable lie." Perhaps I should change that to say, "Men who just aren't any good at lying." I have found that the men I see with mother complexes are no good at lying. But in order for me to explain my reasons, you need to have some fundamental knowledge of developmental psychology.

From the viewpoint of developmental psychology, it is important that a child "tell a lie." It has almost the same importance in meaning as learning to speak. Let me explain in more detail.

To a newborn child, the world is made up of the harmonious relationship between himself and his mother. However, at the very beginning of the developmental stage, he is unable to distinguish between his self and his mother. This is the stage before he becomes aware of himself as an individual.

From this point, little by little, he begins to develop and vaguely begins to become aware that he and his mother exist separately. He also learns that his mother is not the entire world, but only a small part of that world. After that, he becomes aware that he is an independent person. There is some individual variation in the time schedule for this, but in general, awareness of oneself as an individual happens between six months and two years.

The hypothesis that children "live in a daydream" is different from this kind of lie and is extremely important to psychological development. To be able to live in a daydream means that one has the ability to recognize a fantasy world and enjoy it. Children know that the fantasy world is a lie, but use it as a provision to grow and develop.

Lies told by children always begin with lies to their mother.

When they realize that their mother is a separate being from themselves a child then possesses the ability to tell a lie to the mother. However, if they lack the ability or awareness to acknowledge that their mother is a totally separate entity from themselves, then they will never be able to tell a lie to her.

In addition, if they pass the natural developmental stage where it is natural to lie to their mother without developing this ability, they become unable to do anything but live in a symbiotic relationship with their mother. Living symbiotically causes a great deal of damage to one's development. When a mother's influence is too strong, the child becomes very weak. Of course, this influence often remains even after the child attains adulthood.

Think about the men around you who have "mother complexes." You may notice that they are sometimes ridiculously honest and very poor at telling a lie. Men who did not learn to lie to their mothers when they were children have trouble telling lies to their friends, girlfriends, or superiors at work.

THE DIFFERENCE BETWEEN REALITY AND IMAGE

If you are an avid golfer, you may have heard of or read about pro Jack Nicklaus's image training. Nicklaus has said, "Fifty percent of my plays are supported by image training," meaning he visualizes his best shots over and over again in his head. When he does that, he says that he can make great shots at a tournament.

I myself am not a golfer. I came across this story in a book by the brain physiologist Dr. Shinagawa called *Methods of Image Training*. I also found a story about a top rifle shooter who was unable to practice at all for a period of one year, but continued image training by visualizing in his head a bullet hitting the dead center of the target. In spite of the fact that he did no actual training, he came away with first place at a world tournament. Even though he was unable to actually physically train for this event, just doing this image training had the same effect as actual training.

How does image training really work?

It works because the human brain actually lacks the ability to distinguish between reality and image. It isn't just that human knowledge and recognition ability is so vague, but the human brain's ability to sharply distinguish between reality and image is at an extremely low level. In other words, because they are so indistinct, complicated aspects of reality are reduced to a pattern and then recognized.

The fact that the human brain fails to distinguish accurately between reality and images is know experientially by all of us. If you imagine eating a lemon or pickled plum, your mouth begins to secrete saliva. Your brain is reacting to the image of something sour and orders the salivary glands to start producing saliva. Even though it is just an image that you are producing in your mind, from a physiological point of view, the influence extends to the physical level.

When I asked another psychiatrist about this he said, "It is effective to visualize something, but if you also physically make a movement close to what you are visualizing you can get even better results."

If you are visualizing a golf shot, then you should take the same stance as you would use to make the shot and pretend you are holding a golf club. As you visualize the swing, move your hand with it. In addition, if you imagine that the ball is flying high out into the air, your results should be even better. If you do the movement along with the visualization, then your brain becomes even more unable to distinguish between reality and the image. Then the memory of the image will also become more distinct. This is why the effect becomes better.

If you can put to practical use the innate fuzziness that we possess, then it is possible to create real reaction and response just from using visualization.

IF YOU BRAG ABOUT IT,
IT WILL BECOME TRUE

I once read a story about the hotel baron Hilton. When Hilton was young he worked as a bellhop at a small hotel. However, he had bigger dreams, including one day owning his own hotel and being the president of it.

Because of this ludicrous dream, Hilton was nicknamed "president" by his fellow bellhops. Not a single person around him would have ever guessed that he would indeed grow up to be such a famous hotel baron. They all just thought of him as a braggart.

But Hilton really did become a hotel baron.

Of course, he worked very hard, and also had a certain amount of luck to account for his success. There were many ingredients that combined to lead to his success. But, I believe that the biggest element that helped him to fulfill his dream was his persistence in that dream itself. He told his dream to everyone around him and struggled to fulfill it at every moment.

In general, the larger your dreams and ideals are, the more aware you become of your own smallness. People who have big dreams sometimes look at their own smallness and become discouraged.

In fact, it seems to me that the origin of most

people's depression or discouragement is based on this gap between big dreams and the smallness of oneself. To work hard both night and day without giving up in order to realize a huge dream requires an uncommon amount of spiritual strength. Most people become afraid of the size of their own dreams and end up running away from them.

However, if you don't hold on to your dreams, you will lose them. If you throw them away before they become reality, they have no value as dreams. Then they are merely the dregs of dreams.

Hilton is not alone in having had a dream when he was young. Almost all of the founding presidents of businesses had a fantasy when they were young that they worked toward fulfilling. Most of them would be considered a bit reckless, and yet they did not hesitate to share their impossible dreams with the people around them.

If you, too, have some kind of big dream, try sharing it with others. The people around you may just laugh it off. But if you can use their ridicule to motivate you, then you will have that much more reason to realize your dream.

Let Those Around You Be the Teachers

There are always those kind of people around us who seem to "know it all." They are anxious to tell other people what to do. Human beings are prone to wanting to be more competent and stand above others, so it is inevitable that we often meet up with these "know-it-alls." Unfortunately, there seem to be too many of these types in the world and we get sick and tired of them.

The condition of being a "know-it-all" is totally unrelated to age. There are just as many young people who have it as older people. It is not necessarily a result of having had much experience in life, either. In fact, sometimes, the opposite correlation seems to be true. There are many people, who although they are very inexperienced in the ways of the world, still excessively push their views on others.

It is safe to say that people who have the "know-it-all" disease lose out close to 100% of the time. Most people around them do not think well of them at all. Contrary to what they strive for, know-it-alls don't even realize this!

A "know-it-all" is one of the worst kind of things a businessman or a person engaged in commerce can be.

You can usually identify a know-it-all, becuasee they're usually saying something like this.

"What? You didn't even know about that?"

"Let me explain to you just exactly what this is."

"Well, of course you should do it like that. Even a kid would be able to figure that out."

"This is absolutely the way to go. If you bought anything other than this, it would be a total loss."

The "know-it-all's" terrain is not just limited to words. In his very attitude he makes himself appear to be above others, and puts on airs of importance. This too causes discomfort among people around him. It is particularly annoying to see a very young person acting like this.

Human beings like to think for themselves and base their actions on what they have worked out on their own. People who think that "this is something I thought up myself" are able to work in a more positive and productive manner. By contrast, those who have their actions forced upon them by another person, even if they had been thinking of doing just exactly the same thing, take no joy in those actions. That is because another person's will is intervening. It is no longer something decided by one's own judgment.

Smart businessmen are completely familiar with this aspect of human nature. They make sure to never push their own ideas upon others. They take the exact opposite attitude of a "know-it-all." You'll hear them say things like:

"Is that right? I had no idea."

"So, you think I should do it that way? Yes, I see. That's a good explanation."

"Well, I still have a lot to learn. I hope you'll keep me informed about these things."

In this way, the smart person lets others teach him.

Do you see my point here? Even though you may want to be telling somebody what to do, you should hold back those feelings and let the other person tell you what to do. When you do that, the germs of the "know-it-all" disease that lie dormant inside of that person will well up and begin to grow. This is your chance. Let him tell you everything that he wants to tell you. After he is finished telling you what he knows, he will feel a sense of self-respect and satisfaction with himself. At this point he is also ripe for listening to your business proposals.

If he says to you, "You didn't even know about *that?*" and you feel angry and want to make some retort, don't. Don't even show it on your face.

This is an important thing, though there are many businessmen who are totally indifferent to it. They don't even try to listen to the opinions of others. Because of that, their knowledge does not increase. In the end, they will be left behind in the dust.

Perhaps I am showing some signs of this disease myself, as I go on and on writing about it. I should listen to my own lesson!

IF YOU ACT SUCCESSFUL, YOUR WORK WILL GO WELL

When I talk with a salesman who's had a long career, I get the impression that he "loves people." This is probably keeping in character with the job. Most salesmen like to talk and are extroverts.

But when I talk with them further, I often discover that many of them will say something like, "At first I couldn't stand having to meet with so many people." I'd always thought that after so many years of selling you get experienced at doing it and you gain confidence and you discover that you enjoy your work. But often this is not the case. One very skilled salesman told me that he deliberately cultivated that attitude.

When he was young he did not want to go into business. He was a so-called "reluctant salesman." What he really wanted to do was to be in the planning or the research department. But the company assigned him to the sales department.

These days, if a person is assigned to a section of the company that they don't like they often quit their job, or look for other work. But this man was of the generation who believed that "the voice of the company is the voice of God." They don't quit their jobs easily. Instead, they put their effort into thinking about how they could make

themselves fit into that job. This is how that salesman thought, and when he went to get some advice from someone in a position above him that
he was friendly with, he was given the following
advice.

Before he went to meet with someone, this person told him, he should take a few minutes to think
about and imagine that the sales meeting went
smoothly and that the pitch would go well. This
too is a kind of image training, though many salesmen instinctively use these techniques. He too put
this method into action.

At first, he still felt very nervous whenever he
had to visit a customer. But even so, while he sat in
the train on the way to the meeting he would visualize the smiling face of the person in charge in the
conference room and a scene where he was able to
speak fluently of their sales items to the customer.
Gradually his nerves would settle and he would feel
better. After many years of doing this he was surprised to see how much easier it became to meet
with people.

He has tried to explain this technique of doing
things to younger people in his company. But these
men, mostly in their early twenties, tell him,
"Come on, we just want to relax on the train."
They don't want to have to think about work all
the time. Although they have that attitude, it is
these same men who often complain to him when

they are out drinking together that they "really want to get transferred to the advertising section."

Although he was able to change himself successfully, this salesman has yet to find a way to get his young coworkers to change.

HOW TO GET ALONG WITH THE BOSS

There are three elements to doing business well: reports, contact, and talking it over. If these three elements are all firmly in place, then communication within a company will proceed smoothly and work will be successful.

However, there are many young businesspeople who slack off on these things and are thinking of how to get out of being reprimanded so often. A young businessman who works in the sales department of a company selling large-sized computers told me the following method.

In this company too, reports, contact and talking things over are considered to be extremely important. Upper management takes every chance possible to grab people below them and demand to know how things are going. "How are sales talks with Company A going?" "Are you getting close to closing the contract with Company B?"

There are those workers who answer these questions honestly, "Well, it doesn't look too good" or "We've reached an impasse."

When they hear a negative report like this, most managers will then start to blame the worker. "What have you been doing? This isn't what we pay you to do!" But the young businessman that I mentioned before answers those questions this way: "I think that with one more visit I'll get them to sign" or "I'm going to go through the fine print just one more time with them," etc. Even if the prospective customer doesn't seem like he is going to buy the computer, he lies and reports back that there still is a chance of a sale.

If the report given is positive in nature then upper management will have no reason to blame him. Instead, they are likely to encourage him saying something like, "I see, well hang in there with it and good luck." In the end, if no sale is made, he will get reprimanded either way. But a businessman who gives a negative report back while the sales talk is still going on will be reprimanded many times. If you give a report with a positive outlook then you will be reprimanded just once at the end.

When I heard this story, I thought that actually his report was not totally a lie. If there is no possibility at all of a sale, to report back that there may be is definitely a lie. But, you can also look at this story from another point of view.

The other point of view is based in industrial psychology and involves workplace morale. Morale in this case has to do with the will to work and the will to fight for success. It means the group morale.

The reason that upper management reprimands a worker when hearing a report that "it doesn't look like it will sell" is not just because he is concerned about the computer itself. What he is really angry about is the negative and weak attitude of his worker. Negative words such as "can't," or "impossible" are a big no-no to a competitive department such as sales. If there is even one member of the group who says this kind of thing, then a negative mood may prevail over the whole division. For management, the words "can" or "will work out with a little effort" are what they need to hear to keep up a positive atmosphere in the workplace, even if it isn't entirely accurate.

By the way, even in the end, when that salesman had to report back that he didn't make the sale, he had yet another method to keep from being blamed.

"When I have to report back that I have failed, I always ask for advice on how to approach the next prospective customer." For example, "I have found this new customer, but he wants me to...." And then he asks for some advice. As he is doing this he also chooses this time to mention that he has failed with the last customer. If he presents it in that way, he doesn't get blamed as much.

This salesman finds many new prospective customers in his attempt to avoid being blamed, so actually he is quite honestly and legitimately getting good results.

DETECTIVE COLUMBO'S TRAP

I personally believe that most of the top people in the financial world are open-hearted and frank. If they didn't have that kind of personality, it would be difficult for them to make cool decisions under pressure and time constraints.

But I think there is also another reason. For example, there is the case of the founder of Honda Motor Company, Mr. Soichiro Honda.

Mr. Honda would often say that "there is nothing as scary in this world as my mother." He would say this to workers inside the company as well as out in public. He probably didn't say this with any specific intention, but thanks to this open and defenseless speech, the people around him would feel like he was "one of the people."

People feel secure around somebody who is open and seemingly unguarded. At times, it even throws them off their guard. "I don't have to worry about him putting anything over on me" they think, and they lose their wariness. Furthermore, they tend to say things that they normally would be too embarrassed to say. Men in top positions like Mr. Honda are often like this. His "salt of the earth" image helps him appear trustworthy and makes him popular. This honesty and open-heartedness of people in the financial world is an absolutely necessary tool for creating harmony among people, both inside and outside of the company.

It is also possible to use this technique in another way. Just think of Peter Falk in the TV series "Columbo."

Detective Columbo, a competent member of the homicide department, appears in a shabby raincoat driving a car that looks ready for the dump heap. When he begins to question people in a case, he is unable to remember any of the important facts of the matter without constantly consulting his notes. After he finishes questioning a person and has started to walk away, he always immediately comes back once more claiming that he has forgotten to ask something important.

With these numerous flaws working against him, few realize that he is actually an experienced professional who possesses unusually shrewd powers of observation, logical thinking, and the persistence to get to the bottom of the case, along with the energy to investigate every detail. Because of this, even a very mindful suspect will eventually make a slip in front of him.

People like to believe that they are competent, do not make mistakes, and are afraid of nothing. But in some cases having a few visible flaws can work to your benefit in disarming those around you.

HOW TO MAKE SOMEONE SAY WHAT YOU WANT THEM TO SAY

Let's say somebody is talking about his wife and says, "My wife is the worst. Her cooking is lousy and she hates to have sex." If you show an exaggerated sympathetic response such as, "Is that right? What a horrible wife. So your marriage is a failure, huh?" in most cases he will answer by saying, "Well, it isn't all that bad," and say the opposite of what he was originally saying.

By contrast, if you were to say something in response such as, "But I've heard that you have a great wife" and deny what he is saying, then he will most probably become very determined and convince you of it even more. "Not true at all. The other day when I was out drinking and got back a little late, you won't believe what she did...." He will start giving concrete examples to back up his point. This will be the response of almost all people in this situation.

The psychology of human beings is very complex. Just because you praise someone does not mean that he will be happy with your words. Agreeing with someone won't necessarily make a person feel secure. In order to work with this very complicated psyche, it is necessary to have a lot of life experience. However, if you observe very carefully a person's reactions to what you say, and their behavior and expressions when you finish, it is comparatively easy to read their state of mind. If you make it a habit to try and do this all the time, you too can become skilled at human relationships.

THE SECRET TO MAKING A HUNDRED SALES CALLS IN ONE DAY

There is a car dealership near where I live with a very successful salesman. It is said that he can call on one hundred prospective customers in one day.

Just that alone may not be surprising, but I hear that he can finish off these 100 impromptu sales visits in just two hours. That is to say, he can hand out a box of 100 of his business cards in just slightly over 100 minutes. Doing this, he can find prospective customers in just a short time. He uses the rest of his time to devote his sales pitch to those customers who just need a final push before they are ready to sign the contract.

Most people wonder, "How can he possibly do any business in such a short time?" Naturally so. Just the act of knocking on the door and calling out to the potential customer or shop owner who answers and then explaining why he is there could take four or five minutes. Probably there are many people who at this point would refuse to take his business card, so it is almost impossible to imagine that he could go through a whole box of them in just two hours.

But he has a special technique that he has developed to get around this.

When he bursts into a shop he goes right up to the shop owner and says in a very friendly manner, "Hi there, how are you doing?" as he hands him his business card. Then he quickly says the following.

"I remember that the last time we talked you told me that you were thinking of buying a new car in the near future." In fact, this is the first time he is calling on this person so he really has no idea whether or not this person is thinking of buying a new car. But he uses this line to draw the person in. The shopkeeper has many people in and out of his store everyday. Certainly many salesmen stop by. So he really doesn't remember whether or not he has met this guy. The salesman is using that blind point cleverly. If the shopkeeper says, "Oh yeah. I think we did talk about that before" and seems interested, he goes into his sales pitch.

And, if the shopkeeper says to him, "What are you talking about? We aren't buying any new car" then he quickly responds, "Oh really? I guess I must have the wrong store" and is out the door. With this method, he can find a prospective customer in just a one minute call. Just a very small lie like this can create a new opportunity.

Chapter 5
LIES MAKE THE
WORLD GO ROUND

LIES TO DISCOVER THE TRUE FEELINGS
OF A CHEATER

What is the worst kind of lie that can be told between a man and a woman? Excluding those con artists who are motivated by crime, I think that the worst kind of lies are those told by married men to women whom they are interested in fooling around with.

"Things have been cool between us for ages. We even have separate bedrooms."

Men say this kind of thing to make young women feel sympathetic towards them. For the young woman involved, no other lie has the power to make her feel so deceived and foolish. She realizes that the man is just looking for an affair. If he had told her the truth, she would never have gotten involved with him, so he tells this rather conventional lie for reasons of expediency.

Is there a way to see through lies told by lowlifes like this? I would like to introduce all the examples that I can here. But I first want to make it clear that these do not come from my experience. It is an acquaintance of mine, who is quite a playboy, who received this retaliation from a young woman whom he had lied to. He was totally disheartened.

This young woman he was fooling around with was a very bright and beautiful woman (he says). He was interested in her the very first time he laid eyes on her. After going out on a few dates, he told the above lie to get her more intimately involved with him. She fell for this just once. The second time he approached her, she said to him, "Okay, next Sunday, I want you to let me watch you from a distance when you go out shopping with your wife. I promise not to approach you or say anything."

This put him in a perilous position indeed.

If he was really thinking about divorcing his wife, this kind of request wouldn't bother him all that much. If in fact she did come up to them and say something, it would just help the divorce go that much quicker. Or, if he really trusted this young woman one hundred percent, he would be able to believe that she wouldn't approach his wife, and then too, there would be no problem.

But, on the other hand, if he was lying about the

relationship between him and his wife, this request of hers would be quite a psychological burden to him.

First of all, because he had a guilty conscience about telling a lie himself, he would naturally be suspicious that she too was telling a lie. The thought that if she really was lying to him he could be risking his peaceful home life caused him a great deal of mental anguish. He was unable to give an immediate yes or no answer to her. That hesitation was noted by the woman, and the lie was quickly and easily discovered. My playboy friend found himself unable to give her any kind of answer at all, and as she looked at him, she smiled faintly.

In this case it seems that the woman was one or two steps ahead of the game. She had pretended to be fooled by his lies and was herself just enjoying the affair for what it was.

YOU CAN MAKE YOURSELF ACT SINCERE

Lying is closely connected with acting or performance. I can look at my own actions and see this connection for myself.

When a psychiatrist or a counselor interacts with a patient, personal rapport plays a fundamental role, just as it does in any other relationship between human beings. When a patient confides in me I must convey the fact that I am listening to his words very earnestly.

When I think about this, I always wonder to myself about just what exactly sincerity is. Perhaps our interactions in society are really made up of performances that are actually quite distant from the truth.

This is not just a problem for psychiatrists and counselors. The performance factor intervenes for ministers and teachers, businessmen, in relations between lovers and family members, and indeed in every relationship that exists between human beings. Sincerity, or rather conveying sincerity to the other person, is nothing more or less than a lie based on acting. It seems very paradoxical, but there is some truth to this.

In order to improve the effectiveness of performance, calculated lies must be skillfully inserted here and there in human relationships. In a wider sense, it is impossible for us to escape lying as we perform our various roles in the course of everyday life.

Let's imagine a man who is trying to convey his sincerity and depth of his love to a woman. But he is very unskilled at expressing himself. When he awkwardly tries to express his love to her, what kind of impression will she receive from his facial expression and his words?

Nothing strikes a person's heart like the expression of simple artless sincerity. And if he is lucky, then that will do it....

But, when this very timid young man tries to declare his love, his lack of confidence shows in his tone of voice. Even though deep in his heart he is thinking "I love you more than anyone else in the world" he is unable to say it convincingly. This is very natural for him and reflects his style of sincere love, but for the woman listening to him she may wonder "does he really love me all that much? Then why is he so awkward and nervous?"

With this kind of situation there may be no happy ending.

The sincerity that we have is in a wide sense supported by a lie and its performance. In order to convey our sincerity effectively to one another, it is necessary to use simple, but carefully prepared, lies.

CREATING A GAP IN COMMUNICATION

When you are having trouble getting somewhere in a relationship and want to make it deeper than it is, it may be effective to change the rhythm of the communication. This method is particularly effective in a relationship that has begun to get stale with age.

For example, after you have spent one week telephoning every single night, try cutting off all communication for a period of one week. Using this method can sometimes help reel in a person who has been reluctant to make a commitment.

A person who has been the recipient of one week of fervent love calls will begin to feel some amount of security in the relationship. "He really loves me a lot. I don't have to worry about his feelings at all."

Yet if the phone calls suddenly cease, that feeling of security starts to crumble. "Maybe he's getting sick of me." Even though last week the person felt secure and loved, they are now suddenly insecure. At this point a woman must now show her interest in *you*.

In fact, members of the *yakuza*, or Japanese gangsters, often use this method when they are trying to snare a woman to be their mistress. Of course, their method is more vicious.

When they first approach the woman whom they have targeted, they come across as very deferential to her. If she has some complaint they listen endlessly, nodding in agreement. They never say anything critical like "You're the one who is wrong." The woman feels secure and thinks, "This guy really cherishes me a lot."

When he has her thinking that way, suddenly the man distances himself from her. He begins to dodge her calls, saying he has stuff to do for the gang, or that he has to meet with the guys. At that point he has her thinking, "I can't live without him."

LIES TO GET TO KNOW SOMEONE

Sometimes telling a bold lie, even to the point of being reckless, can bring about excellent results. This story involves a man now in his fifties.

When this man was in this twenties he really wanted a girlfriend. He had already experienced a number of relationships, but he didn't yet feel satisfied. He was greedy and wanted to be with a large number of women. However, back in those days, there was no easy way to go on a "girl hunt." Nor were there any places like discos where young people could easily meet up with one another. So, this man thought up the following tactic.

First of all, he looked up the telephone number of a dormitory at a woman's college. On Sunday morning, he would make a call to this dormitory and say the following.

"May I speak to Miss Saito?"

It didn't have to be "Miss Saito." It could have been "Miss Yamada" or "Miss Tanaka." He simply picked a common enough name so that there would be sure to be one or two women of that name in the dormitory. When the girl picked up the phone he would say:

"This is so-and-so. Remember, we met the other day, and now I'm calling to see if you want to go out today."

Of course this was a completely made-up story. Most of the women would be puzzled or a little suspicious and ask, "Where is it that we met?" According to him, this was the crucial point at whether or not he would be successful.

"What? Have you forgotten? You know, it was in that coffee shop near campus. What's it called again? Remember, we were talking about that movie and all kinds of things. You really don't remember?"

This too was totally made up. Since they had never met of course the woman had no recollection of meeting. But as he went on talking, surprisingly, one out of three of the young women would end up agreeing to meet with him, he says. Probably, it wasn't that they really believed that they had forgotten where they'd met, but rather that it was a Sunday and they had nothing better to do and were curious. Rather than just being bored in the dormitory, they decided to take a chance on meeting him.

What he did next was even trickier.

After giving her the name of the coffee shop where they would meet, he would get her to tell him what she would be wearing that day. Then he would arrive at the coffee shop early. He would nonchalantly keep his eye on the door, and when the woman appeared he would decide whether or not he wanted to meet her. If she was attractive he would get up to greet her, but if she wasn't attractive he would quietly leave the shop.

To the "unattractive" young women who fell for this, it was indeed an annoyance, but it's just one example of how people use lies to meet people.

WHY DO PEOPLE FALL FOR CON ARTISTS?

There are countless con artists who quite cleverly play on the emotions of a woman's heart. When we look at their *modus operandi* we can see one point that they all have in common. They work in extremely short time frames from the first meeting until the marriage proposal. If the time they spend courting one woman is too long, then the "efficiency of investment" will be poor, so I suppose that this is only natural. But, even so, I am dumbstruck at the speed at which they work.

One extreme example is that of a woman who was picked up by a man at a movie theater. After the movie, they went to a coffee shop, where the man proposed marriage to her. Of course the woman said no, but the man forcibly returned to her home with her and roughly pursued a physical relationship with her. The next morning, he said to her, "Let's go meet my parents in Hokkaido" and got her to pay for the tickets. In order to reassure the woman who looked uneasy at handing over the money, he called to send a telegram to his parents saying, "Coming home with fiancée."

All con artists work quickly like this. Besides the "efficiency of investment" factor described above, the main reason they work quickly is to keep the woman confused and cloud her power of judgment.

Con artists are able to intuitively search out those women who wish desperately to get married. This is not to say that they are mind readers. They prey on women who are alone at movie theaters or restaurants, or are otherwise looking lonely. Some go so far as to put up a shingle as a marriage advisor so that they can seduce unsuspecting young women.

When they find such a woman, they first try to give the impression that they are a truly caring and loving man so they can gain her trust. Before their true identity can be discovered, they quickly propose. The young woman does not absolutely trust him at this point, but with this sudden and bold proposal in front of her, she loses her chance to say that "something is strange here." This state of confusion is just what he is aiming for.

When a human being's heart is in a state of confusion it is impossible to make cool and objective decisions. If they have known each other for just a few short months when the man proposes, it is impossible for her to weigh all his good and bad points and come up with a comprehensive picture. A sudden proposal does not allow for a cool decision. The desire to be happily married that has long been in her heart rules her emotions and she falls right into the trap.

Almost all women think that "I'd never fall for a con artist; I'm too smart for that." But this is just when they are calm and collected. There are few women who can maintain this cool judgment when a "knight in shining armor" comes riding up in front of them.

In addition to all of this, con artists are surprisingly skillful in the way that they use money around the women whom they target. They know the weak points of a woman's psyche, and use money in a way that the average man could never think of. After all, to them it is a kind of "investment" so they have learned the most effective way to use their money.

IF SOMEONE LIES TO YOU

What is the best thing to do if you discover that you have been lied to? If the lie involves a crime, then of course the best thing to do is to immediately report it to the police. But what if it is just a small lie made to you by an acquaintance?

In this case, our immediate response may be to

confront the person directly. But if you do that, you will not find out why the person lied to you in the first place. It is better to first get to the bottom of what is really going on and to carefully find out all that you can before you make any judgments.

Unless a person is a chronic liar, there is always a reason for telling a lie. It may be from pride, or to cover their tardiness, or some other specific reason. In that case you don't need to find out much more. If you want to accuse them of lying then you can go ahead, and if you want to let it go, you can just let them go on lying. There won't be much actual harm done in any case.

However, if you have a more serious type of relationship in which there are larger interests involved, the reasons a person may be telling a lie are more complex. In this case, it isn't wise to jump right in and make accusations. If you remain silent and let the person think that his lie has succeeded you can observe carefully to see what will happen next. This is a better plan than direct confrontation.

It is possible that he knows that you know he has lied. Or there may be some very special circumstances making him nervous and causing him to lie. If that is the case, he will be very grateful to you for being magnanimous enough to let him get away with his lie. And because of that he may never tell a lie again.

We must also consider that he may have lied out of malice. However, even in this case, there is no sense in exposing him at the first stage of it. The next time he will probably come up with a more skillful lie and try to dodge his way through with that. In this case, it is better to first let him get away with a small lie, in order to find out what his intention is in telling the lie.

When he is feeling reassured that he has gotten away with lying, he may next tell an even more blatant lie. It won't be too late to make accusations then. By this time, you will probably have gathered enough proof so that he cannot deny it.

IF YOU CAN'T SAY IT, SHOW IT
THROUGH BODY LANGUAGE

When you meet someone new and have the impression that he is "hard to deal with," chances are this person is thinking the same thing about you. In the business world, you can't afford the luxury of thinking this way. No matter how you may feel about someone personally, if you don't make an effort to create smooth communication you may find it adversely affects your working relationships. At times like this, "posture echoing" is a good technique to try to ease communication.

Just as the words suggest, "posture echoing" means to take on the same posture as the other person, to put your body in the same position.

For example, if the other person folds his arms, then you should also fold your arms. If he begins to stroke his cheek, then you also raise your hand to do the same. And if he crosses his legs or puts his hand to his head you continue to mirror his actions. Of course, if you are too obvious about your actions you will end up making him uneasy, so you must do it a few seconds behind him in an unobtrusive manner.

It is effective to copy his movements as well as his posture. If he starts to drink his tea, then you pick up your cup as well. If he lights up a cigarette then take out one yourself. If you match your movements to his, then it "appears to be" that you are in sync with each other.

This "appears to be" is a very important point.

It is very rare that two people are ever totally in sync with each other from the very beginning. In most cases, unless they are extremely compatible, people ordinarily feel some wariness towards each other. A certain amount of time is necessary to unravel that wariness. But if you use this "posture echoing" it is possible to unravel this wariness much more rapidly.

Human communication is not just established based on words. It is expressed through the whole body including one's words.

Love, or intimacy, can be expressed by casually copying the movements of the other person. Conversely, when you want to extricate yourself from talking with a disagreeable person you can purposely act just the opposite of the other person. He will soon get the idea.

In the business world, there are many cases when you cannot tell a verbal lie. But lying with body language is no problem at all.

EVEN IF YOU DISAGREE, FIRST AGREE

People tend to get very heated up when they get into a discussion. Debates in the business world are particularly susceptible to emotions since they involve each person's own interests. The stakes may be tremendous. When your adversary persists in his own way of thinking and you too have no intention of budging, the situation reaches an impasse. A defiant position on your part will only add fuel to the fire and increase his defiance as well. When you have reached this point, it becomes almost impossible to come to terms no matter what kind of reasonable compromise plan is suggested.

Veterans of debate never stupidly stick to their

own views. They nod in agreement as they listen to the other person's opinion. After letting the other person go on about how he wants things done, they end up getting their own way in the end. It appears to be magic, but if I explain the process step-by-step, you will see that this is something anybody can do.

Persons skilled at negotiation always acknowledge the opinion of the other person first. Of course, they really don't want to do this at all. But in order to win, they lie a little. This is not just a pose; it is the first step of a tactical strategy.

When they recognize the other person's opinion it is just as if they are consigning the opinion into the palm of their own hand. You need to have the other person in the palm of your hand before you can manipulate him.

Then you let the other person say all that he wants to say and get it all out. You don't utter a word of disagreement until he is totally finished. You just listen quietly. If there is some degree of intricacy involved in the discussion then you may occasionally lend a word to keep matters on track, but the important thing is to let him get all he wants to say off his chest. You listen carefully until he has exhausted himself.

"Basically you're right, I agree." Even if you don't agree at all, you must continue nodding in agreement. This is to convince him that you are completely attuned to him.

After he has finished speaking, it is important to not rush in with your opposing opinion. Pros at these kind of talks never "refute," but instead continue talking using questions. It is essential that the questions be formulated so that the other person answers with a "yes." You must absolutely not let the other person say "no." You will entangle him in the end with "yes."

The following is a very simplified example of this method. It involves one person trying to get another person to stop smoking.

"Cigarettes don't just hurt the person who is smoking them. They also cause health problems for the people around them."

"Yes, I've heard that."

"So, when you smoke, you are actually hurting your wife as well."

"Yes, I guess that is true."

"Do you love your wife?"

"Well, yeah, sure."

"When you smoke and it damages your health then your wife is sad, isn't she?"

"Yes, I suppose so."

"And if your wife, whom you say you love, should ever get sick due to your cigarette smoking you would feel awful, wouldn't you?"

"Well....yeah."

"So, you'd be upset, and you really shouldn't be making your wife unhappy, should you?"

"Yeah, you are right again."

"Then you should give up smoking, right?"

"...."

This is of course a very oversimplified example, and you may find it hard to be convinced. But if you can keep getting the other person to say "yes" all along, it will not be difficult to get them to say that final "yes" as well, and win the larger battle.

In order to use this method successfully, it is essential to first acknowledge the person's point of view. Even if it is a lie, you have to say "yes" first. This is a typical example of hiding your true feelings in order to get somebody to do what you want them to do.

Pygmalion is a young man who was a sculptor and appears in Greek mythology.

One day he sculpted his vision of the perfect woman out of marble. When the statue was complete, it was so perfect that he fell in love with it. He gazed at the statue everyday and thought to himself, "If only she would come alive." The goddess Venus, upon observing this, felt pity for the young man and granted him his wish, giving life to the statue. Pygmalion married the statue and supposedly lived happily ever after.

If the feelings and hopes that we have for someone are earnest and strong enough, the other person will fulfill our hopes. This myth attempts to show us the power of our wishes.

If you are middle-aged or older then you will probably remember Bernard Shaw's drama "Pygmalion" and the movie based on that drama called "My Fair Lady." It is the story of Eliza, a Cockney flower girl, who is taken in and educated by Professor Higgins, who then introduces her to society.

In the field of psychology, for a person to have expectations of another and then to put those expectations on that other person and guide them into fulfilling them is called the "Pygmalion effect," after the Greek myth. All people are looking to be praised; it's one of the fundamental needs of human beings.

Abraham Maslow, who is the former chairman of the American Psychological Association, states four of the five stages of human needs: physiological needs, safety needs, the need for love or belongingness, and lastly, the need for esteem or status. When these needs remain unfulfilled, human beings end up feeling inferior or powerless. This often leads to despair and is even said to be the cause of neurotic behavior. When a person fails to receive recognition not only do they find themselves unable to reach their potential, but there is also some danger of them becoming ill as well.

Because of this, in any kind of situation, it is necessary to acknowledge the other person's point of view in order to get them to react in the way you want them to. When you give them some sort of recognition, then it is best to remember that the ends justify the means and if a lie provides some sort of expediency, you should feel free to tell one.

The last need in Maslow's five stages is the need for self-actualization. That is the need for a person to become the person that he or she wants to be.

In the future, it will not only be necessary to give recognition to the people we deal with, but possibly we should pay attention to this need of our own as well.

SENDING CONFLICTING MESSAGES

If you think of all human relationships as some sort of game, then you begin to want to try some mischief. Of course it isn't good to do anything to hurt a person's feelings, but it could be an interesting experience to gain some understanding of the structure of the psyche by using a small lie to observe the behavior of human beings.

When I say a lie, I'm not only talking about empty words, but a technique which encompasses your attitude as well. This method involves the use of what is called in psychopathology the "double-bind."

The "double-bind" is a concept advocated by Gregory Bateson, the British cultural anthropologist who later immigrated to America to do research in psychiatry. After studying schizophrenics, he concluded that schizophrenia occurred when there was a "social circumstance in which one must cope with contradiction."

For example, let's look at a couple. One of them says to the other, "I love you very much, more than anyone else in the world." But as he says this, his face shows absolutely no sign of love, and his body language is contradictory to his words. Confronted with this kind of behavior, the other person is unable to know whether she is loved or not loved, and becomes very confused. This is a "social circumstance where one must cope with contradiction."

Over time, if you continue to receive contradictory messages, your human consciousness is unable to make any judgment and it is easy to become fragmented. This was Bateson's conclusion. Bateson began his research by observing the relationship between mother and child. Later, other psychiatrists would develop this theory even further, applying it to all family relationships.

A double-bind that you are not aware of is the most difficult to deal with, but it is possible to use this double-bind as a technique in everyday communication.

Let's say you have a lover and the two of you have had an argument. Or, you sense that their feelings are cooling towards you. In this case, try being as nice as you can possibly be for awhile and then heavily criticize them on every fault you can think of. If this sounds a little extreme, then try just ignoring them or pretending lack of interest. If you do this, the other person will not be able to grasp what your true feelings are and will experience some confusion. From that state, the coolness they were beginning to feel towards you will change from curiosity to interest, and then very likely into love.

However, you must be careful not to overdo this. If you do it with no subtlety, you will just be thought of as "someone who plays with people's heads" or "a person who is impossible to understand" and will end up being hated. It is wise to just use this as a kind of tactic to understand the movement of the other person's feelings for you.

LIES FOR LIVING WISELY

A businessman, who had moved from Kansai to Tokyo, once lamented:

"Don't the people in Tokyo know anything about the subtleties of word play? It's so hard to deal with people who take every word at face value."

When he was transferred to the Tokyo area a number of salesmen appeared in his office to try to get some orders from him. He said to the salesmen, as they spread open their catalogues, "Well, I'll give it some thought. Why don't you come back and see me another time." This is how he had always talked to salesmen in Kansai.

For him, this was a way of saying no: "I have no

intention of buying anything. Don't come back." Salesmen in the Kansai area all know that, and when they hear these words they don't come again.

However, salesmen in Tokyo are different. Even though he had, in a roundabout way, turned them down, they would show up at the company again at a later date.

At that point, the businessman would say, "I'll talk to you later." When he repeated these words, some of the salesmen got angry and said to him, "Later, later. When exactly is it that you want me to come?"

At first he didn't understand why these salesmen were getting so angry. In the meantime, his wife at home was having the same experiences with door-to-door newspaper salespeople and car dealers. When they both talked it over together he at last understood: his saying "later" was just a euphemism for "no" to him, but it was taken literally in Tokyo.

Recounting this story reminds me of a famous *rakugo* [8] tale from the Kamigata *rakugo* called "The Bubuzuke of Kyoto."

"Bubuzuke" is a kind of *ochazuke* [9]. In the Kyoto

---

[8] Rakugo is traditional Japanese comic storytelling, which makes heavy use of puns and word play. It is usually performed by professional storytellers.

[9] Ochazuke is rice with tea poured over it, served with either pickles, salted salmon flakes or pickled plums. It is often served as a late night snack or a light meal.

area if a guest comes to visit and then is ready to leave, the host will often say, "Please, don't be in a rush to leave us. Wouldn't you like to eat some bubuzuke?" This is designed to make the guest feel like his presence is desired for even longer. Yet no guest who is native to Kyoto will say, "Yes, I'd love to have some" because they all know that these words are said simply to be polite.

The tale of "The Bubuzuke of Kyoto" is a funny story involving a guest from Osaka who has never heard of bubuzuke and is determined to try it. If you think hard about it, these traditional words are about lies that help to keep human relations running smoothly —they have the wisdom of the times and city life in it. People of Kyoto, who have a thousand-year history of living together in a small valley, are well aware that small lies are necessary in our human society. After all, although they have no intention of buying, they say "come back later." And though they have no intention of cooking it, they offer bubuzuke.

LIES FOR HEALING THE "NOBODY LOVES ME" DISEASE

"I've never met a person I disliked."

These are well-worn words. It is my guess that nobody can say this with complete honesty. When you are forced to deal with strong-minded persons at work, you begin to see the bad points of just about everyone around you. But you should turn the statement around: "There are no people who dislike me." If you can take this kind of philosophical view, then your life will go more smoothly.

I want those of you who are feeling some kind of obstacle in human relationships (particularly those who feel it between men and women) to engrave these words upon your heart. Those of you who constantly feel that "nobody loves me" should chant these words like an incantation before you go to bed or walk out the door to meet anyone.

The "nobody loves me" disease is found mostly in people who are just looking to be the passive recipients of love. Although they themselves do not make the effort to actively give love to someone, they expect to receive affection from others. This is a very immature kind of personality, but one that I have seen quite often lately. And it leads to both depression and insomnia.

If you are not actively giving love and affection out yourself, the chances of receiving it are extremely low. If you try this out in everyday life, you will soon realize the truth of it.

For example, let's say you enter a coffee shop. A student who works there part time brings you over some water and an *oshibori*. [10] If you bark out your

10 A small steaming hot towel given to customers at coffee shops and other restaurants to wipe their hands on before eating.

order with a snarl on your face, shouting "Coffee!" chances are your waiter will slam the coffee cup down in front of you roughly. [11]

On the other hand, if you say politely, "I'd like some coffee, please" not only will he bring you your coffee and put it down quietly, he will probably also be smiling. Of course there are those waiters who are just unfriendly by nature so this doesn't always hold true, but if you try it out several times you will see that I am right.

You can't receive love and affection by being passive. Even if it seems to work at first, if you are always the passive one, the affection will not last long. It is necessary for you to return that affection for the relationship between the two of you to deepen.

If you are a person who is worried about "not being loved" then you should repeat those famous words to yourself over and over. At first it may seem like an obvious lie to you, but if you keep on repeating it you will gradually begin to understand the importance and truth of these words.

When that happens, true love will not be far behind.

---

[11] In Japan, there is no tipping at restaurants, so customer service is not influenced by this factor.

Chapter 6
AFTER YOU TRANSCEND
A LIE, YOU CAN SEE
THE TRUTH

SEEING THE REAL TRUTH

An interesting experiment was once done by an American woman named Grace Halsell. This woman is a pure Caucasian, but through the use of chemicals, she was able to dye her skin black. Her goal was to study societal behavior based on her skin color. Ms. Halsell says that what she first felt when she disguised herself as a black woman was sexual fear. That is to say, she became aware of the sexual violence that white men have towards black women. She found that as a black woman she experienced a kind of harassment from white men that she had never felt as a white woman.

This kind of experiment can wake us up to the fact that usually we human beings are only aware of a very limited reality. We only see things through the perspective of the group we ourselves are a part of in society. If we change our position, we can see a whole other world around us, but we are usually unable to take even the first step into that world.

Another example, similar to this, is that of a German journalist who joined up with Turkish seasonal workers to do an exposé on the conditions of the lowest class of workers in Germany. There are also freelance writers here in Japan who have joined the ranks of seasonal workers in automobile factories in order to write about worker conditions. These writers have experienced a whole different world than they would have as white collar workers leading comfortable lives.

These are all quite serious examples. On the lighter side, we have the example of the popular television drama "Mito Komon." Disguised as just another old man, the hero is able to punish corrupt magistrates who have run amuck.

If you think that you want to uncover a hidden truth, don't make the stupid mistake of trying to confront the issue head on. It is necessary to lower your focus to the lowest possible point. If you do this, you may be able to see the truth most unexpectedly.

BODIES DON'T LIE

Ways of searching out the truth have been studied since ancient times. One extreme method of finding the truth out is torture. Many different means of torture have been invented and continue to be used in some countries even today.

Since torture is outlawed in most modern countries, more research has been done in humane methods of finding out the truth. One example of this is the device known as the lie detector.

Police were able to affirm that it was Dr. N who killed his wife and three children in Tsukuba by using a lie detector on him. Dr. N was a very cautious man and was highly educated and elite. But he couldn't fool the lie detector.

The physiological index of a human being changes when confronted by mental anguish or excitement. The heart rate and electrodermal activity change. The sweat glands in the palms of the hands, soles of the feet, and under the arms are stimulated and put on guard; a change in the emotional state is always accompanied by excitement. Excitement occurs in the hypothalamus of the diencephalon and the cerebrum cortex. It is thought that messages pass through the sympathetic nerves and reach the sweat glands of the cells. If a person is lying about something extremely important, they will start to sweat inside (emotional sweating).

Although we can tell a verbal lie, our bodies will usually not lie. By analyzing these changes it is possible to judge whether or not a lie is being told. Electrodes similar to those used for electrocardiograms are attached to the palms and wrists of the hands. About three volts of electricity are sent directly through the body. The amount of current is so subtle that the testee is unable to feel it. The polygraph will react when they listen to music, feel some pain, or are asked to do mental calculations. These reactions also occur when they feel ashamed, or if they have an image of something disagreeable in their head.

Lie detector results cannot be used as admission of proof, but they can be very useful at the investigative stages. In Japan the Science Investigative and Research Bureau does research on lie detectors, and they have been authorized for use by the police.

In America, in addition to being used in almost all of the investigations of serial killers, the lie detector is also used in business personnel departments to check for loyalty. The lie detector is used in a much broader way there than in Japan.

There are flaws with the lie detector procedure. Anybody has a right to refuse to be tested, and in some rare cases, a very cool and collected murderer who has no sense of guilt over his actions can appear to be innocent when he is questioned using this lie detector. Dr. Hannibal Lecter in the movie "Silence of the Lambs" would surely appear as innocent. By contrast, Dr. N reacted with very normal emotions and behavior.

LIES EXPOSED BY THE "COCKTAIL PARTY" EFFECT

Let's imagine ten or so people get together at a function and are noisily enjoying themselves. When ten or more people get together, they tend to break up into a few small groups. Each group is speaking boisterously and, if there is alcohol served, the atmosphere is probably quite lively.

Recently at an event like this I was talking to the man next to me and passing on some gossip about a friend of ours. I wasn't speaking in a loud voice. In fact, since it was just the two of us talking, I was actually speaking in a very subdued voice. Everyone else around us was caught up in their own conversations so I didn't think there was any possibility of being overheard.

However, just as I said something slightly derisive about a friend who was present in the room, I heard his voice from across the table—

"Hey! What bad things are you saying about me now?"

To tell the truth, I was very surprised. It wasn't very nice of me to be speaking ill of him, but I had no idea he would be able to pick up on what I was saying in that very noisy room.

This is a phenomenon which has been called the "cocktail party effect."

At cocktail parties, many people gather and the atmosphere is loud and lively. If you speak in a low voice it should be almost impossible for other people to pick up on what you are saying. However, in that atmosphere, if the topic being spoken about relates to you then, strangely enough, you are often able to pick up on it. If you have trouble believing this, please go to a bar and try it out. If you go to a bar where there is a pretty woman behind the counter, try speaking to the person next to you in a low voice about her when she is at the other end of the counter speaking with a customer. In most cases she will send an anxious look in your direction indicating that she has heard you.

The same phenomenon can be seen when you are dozing.

Imagine that somebody is dozing, while others are chatting pleasantly in the vicinity. The people who are chatting can hear the even breathing of the person dozing and imagine him fast asleep. They begin to talk about him. Of course even if they are sure he is fast asleep, nobody would speak very frankly in a loud voice with him sleeping right there. Most of the time, they would speak in a low voice if they spoke ill of him.

But no matter where he was off to in dreamland, the person who is dozing will suddenly awake when the topic turns to him. There may be some readers here too who have been in this awkward situation: you may even be unable to admit to being awake and pretend to continue to be asleep.

Lies can be discovered by little slips in these situations. Feeling overly secure about your environment can be a huge downfall when you are telling a lie. No matter how small or trivial a lie you are telling, don't ever tell the real truth in a place where the person involved can overhear it.

"Ignorance is Bliss" Lies

Can hypnosis tell us what is really true? In fact, a person who has been hypnotized is still able to tell a lie, and can also know that they are telling a lie.

Long ago in Europe, officials would accept testimony in court that was given while a witness or defendent was under hypnosis. A woman who had been raped would be hypnotized and they would try to find out who the guilty man was. The results of this were tragic. The woman would testify that she had suffered greatly and most of the men were found to be guilty. But in fact, most of the cases were entirely made up.

It is also thought that being under hypnosis actually makes it easier to tell a lie. A human being's heart is filled with complexities. Just as when you are peeling away the layers of an onion and never seem to reach the core of it, there are layers of fantasy, fiction and deception in the human heart. This must be understood when looking at problems of the heart.

When a person realizes that they have been deceived, what is their common reaction?

The most obvious thing that we can think of is anger. We put aside the possibility of our own carelessness, lack of social common sense, and the depth of our greed, and turn our resentment towards the person who has deceived us. This is a very honest reaction. In a society where we hold assumptions about the goodness of human beings, deception is an act that deserves censure, so it is natural to react with anger.

However, there are some people who react to being deceived by denial. I am more fascinated by this kind of person than by the person who reacts directly with anger.

A woman who has been deceived by a marriage con artist is urged by the people around her to claim damages against the man. But she doesn't. "It's not true. He's not really that kind of person," she says, and refuses to believe that she has been swindled. The real winner in this situation is the con artist himself. Believe it or not, there really are victims who react in this manner.

People who have been swindled by someone appearing to be trading in futures may also have become vaguely aware of the fact that they are being deceived somewhere along the line. Yet they continue to give the swindler more money. It isn't so much that they are victims of their own greed, but rather that they don't want to admit that they have been deceived, usually out of pride.

It is an extremely heavy psychological burden for a human being to admit to being deceived by another human being. In essence it involves admitting to one's own incompetence and lack of smarts.

In the case of a woman who has obviously been swindled by a man, she may not want to sully with the vulgar reality of deception what may have been a beautiful memory of having a man in love with her and wanting to marry her. If she admits that she has been deceived, she loses that memory. For a woman, this reflects on her very identity and is a serious problem. The loss of large amounts of money is not nearly as important to some people as the memory of "just once in my life I have been loved."

We can see something similar to this among the first generation of Japanese immigrants to Brazil. The Japanese immigrants in Brazil can be divided into two groups —the "winners" and the "losers." This division is based on whether or not they will admit that Japan made an unconditional surrender in World War II. A survey done twenty years after the end of the war revealed the surprising fact that eighty percent of the first generation of immigrants believed that Japan had been victorious over the Allied Powers. Some of these Brazilian villages were made up almost entirely of immigrants who believed in Japan's victory, and they actually had chased out the "losers" from the town.

No matter what kinds of arguments were brought forth, the "winners" refused to acknowledge Japan's unconditional surrender. When shown history books and news clips from after the defeat, they merely retorted that the evidence was "an American conspiracy." One "winner" who made a trip back to Japan to visit looked around at all the skyscrapers of Tokyo and was even more convinced that he was right. "Look at how prosperous Japan has become. Would a country that had lost a war be this wealthy?"

The reason that these "winners" cannot acknowledge Japan's defeat is because that if they do acknowledge it then they must admit that their own lives have been in vain. This first generation of immigrants immigrated to Brazil "to help the Japanese Empire." The reason that they worked hard under difficult conditions was all for the sake of their country. If they believed that in spite of their sacrifices Japan was defeated, then they would be forced to question their own decisions and lives over the last fifty years.

Women who have been deceived by men, along

with this group of "winners," both prefer to choose the happiness obtained by continuing to be deceived rather than confront the fact that they have been deceived and face unhappiness.

FAITH IS A LIE TURNED INSIDE OUT

Here is another reaction to being deceived.

The founder of one of the new religions here in Japan made a prediction that "on XX day at XX time in 1988 a major earthquake will strike the Tokyo metropolitan area, causing its destruction." The believers all were thrown into a flurry, and on that day gathered in the suburbs of Tokyo. Up until the very moment when the earthquake was predicted to strike, they prayed together with all of their might for safety and mercy.

In the end, there was no earthquake. Not even a slight tremor was felt in the Tokyo area, and nothing out of the ordinary happened at all.

According to an outsider, who did not believe the words of this founder, the prediction was a meaningless one, and the prayers of the followers had no impact or meaning at all. Whether they prayed or not Tokyo remained the same. If there were some people in Tokyo who knew about the prediction, then their reactions would merely be, "so it turns out he was wrong after all." Most people who heard the prediction had probably forgotten about it by the day it was supposed to occur. (Incidentally, there was a fortune teller who in a certain magazine clearly predicted the Great Hanshin Earthquake.)

However, the point of view of the believers is 180 degrees in opposition. They don't in the least believe that "he was wrong after all." What they believe is that the power of their prayers reached up to the heavens and the earthquake was avoided. When the earthquake failed to occur, generally there were only two choices left to the believers. One was to cut all ties with their leader and give up their religion. Another choice was to believe that "it is because our leader's power is absolute and because our faith is strong that an earthquake was avoided," and to thus strengthen their belief even further. A devoted believer would not hesitate at all when faced with this choice and in fact would not even feel there was a choice here; they'd automatically choose the path towards even more fervent belief.

Even if their leader's prediction had been absolutely correct and an earthquake did occur, the believers would never think that "even though we prayed our hardest we were unable to stop the earthquake, so our leader's belief must be wrong." Instead they would theorize that "our leader was absolutely right in his prediction. This proves that he has divine powers. The reason that this very unfortunate earthquake has occurred is because our faith was not strong enough. We need to pray even harder and be more devoted." Either way, devout believers will always find a path towards strengthening their beliefs.

It is extremely difficult for a human being to abandon something they have chosen to believe in. It is easier to go on searching for reasons proving that a belief is correct than admitting to a mistake in something that you believe in.

In Christian scholastic philosophy there is also a saying that "it is irrational, therefore we believe." This thesis shows directly the relationship between reason and belief; that is, denying reason is the secret to belief. It is interesting to note that not only cults but all universal world religions extol the dogma that the rationality of belief must be absolutely dominant.

HOW DO CHEATERS GET CAUGHT?

Women's magazines often make the claim, "It is hard to know what a man is thinking, but if you can get them to let down the guard on their heart they are much simpler than you think." The guard around a man's heart sometimes appears to be just a lie. If you can see through a man's lies..... There are many women who think this way when agonizing over matters of the heart. As I have said before, lies are always conveyed by attitudes and gestures.

Of course, there are times when a man is playing it both ways. If he is caught fooling around he knows very well what will happen, so he lies frantically. However, the more earnest in his lies he becomes, the more he comes apart at the seams. If you poke at the seams skillfully, than he has no choice but to surrender.

If you let your anger get the best of you and accuse him on the spot of telling a lie, then in most cases the woman will lose. First you must be calm and cool and consider how you can most effectively expose him. Let's look at a few examples that I have gathered from a woman's magazine. These examples will also be useful for a man, so that he doesn't make a mistake like this.

Example 1: He stopped calling me by my name.
He was a twenty-seven-year-old man who worked in the same company as Mariko. He had played basketball in college and was built solidly. He seemed trustworthy—an "older brother" type. He had an easy-going personality and kindly helped Mariko through the ropes when she was first hired at their company. Mariko began going out with him about six months after she started working there. Since he lived by himself, she would go over once every

two weeks and clean his apartment and do his laundry for him. She first became aware of the existence of another woman about a year after they had started going out.

Even though he had always called Mariko by her name, one day he started just calling her "sweetie" or "hon." At first she thought it meant that their relationship had become even more intimate and she was very happy. But one day when she was talking with another women and bragging about this, the woman told her that this meant he was seeing another woman.

In other words, the reason he had stopped calling her by name was so he didn't say the other woman's name by accident. This was his way of covering his tracks. If he did call her by another woman's name, then it would be proof that he had been with another woman.

She then began to look at what he was doing when they weren't on a date. For example, she telephoned the company when he claimed he was working overtime, and telephoned him at home at times when he should have been there. When she did this she found some discrepancies in what he was telling her and many hours that were unaccounted for. Mariko thought to herself, "I'm going to make him confess that he's seeing someone else."

She went to his apartment and purposely dropped an earring there. She pretended to find it

hat's this? It isn't my earring!" For one
ok of distress crossed his face and then
ck to her, "Yeah it is yours." She burst out
d said, "I trusted you..." (Of course they
were not real tears.)

After that, he acted as could be expected. "I'm
sorry. I'll never fool around on you again."

"This time I'll forgive you, but if you ever do it
again, it will be the end of us."

After that she made him promise to always call
her by her name and things went smoothly for them.

Example 2: An expressway receipt gives it away.
Last autumn, Yoshiko took a two-week trip to New
York with one of her friends. When she discussed
the trip with her boyfriend he encouraged her to go
and even drove them to the airport and picked
them up upon their return. Yoshiko thought there
was something strange going on.

Her boyfriend was the jealous type, and when
she told him she was going on this trip she didn't
expect him to be very happy about it. But she some-
how felt a little out of sorts when he was so nice
about it. Immediately she figured that his cheerful
face must be hiding something.

Soon after she returned from New York they
went on a drive to Yokohama. They had lunch in
Chinatown and then spent the night at a romantic
hotel. On the way back, they stopped at a parking

area so that he could use the bathroom. Sitting in the car bored, she happened to open the glove compartment to look at a map. As she was turning the pages, a receipt from another hotel on the expressway fell out. When she checked the date on it, she saw that it was on a day when she had been in New York.

"So, while I was away," Yoshiko thought to herself, "he took advantage of that and was fooling around with another woman. So that is why he was so nice about driving me and picking me up from the airport." She was very angry and she knew that she wouldn't be able to control her words, so she tried to compose herself. She remained silent on the drive home as she planned her next move.

If she stuck the receipt under his nose and demanded to know what it was, it would probably just end in a fight. As far as Yoshiko knew, this was the first time that he had cheated on her and she thought that she could forgive him this time. But, she also thought that she wanted to let him know that she knew about it and put an end to anything like it in the future. So, when she got out of the car, she took the receipt and stuck it under the front wipers of the car. She said to him, "See you later" and went inside to her apartment. She was taking a gamble that he would choose her over the other woman. Two or three days later he called and apologized.

"Your wordless punch was a strong one. This time I was the one who did wrong, so I'm going to take you out and buy you anything that you want."

She thought that she wanted to pay him back by asking him to buy her something really expensive, so she took him with her to a department store and made him buy her a Hermes scarf. It cost close to $400, but he just said, "I promise not to fool around on you anymore, so I hope you'll forgive me." He said that the other woman was just someone that he'd picked up at a bar.

Example 3: He stopped using his credit card.
When Rie was a first year student at a junior college and thinking that she was ready to get married, she discovered that her boyfriend was fooling around on her.

He was a very showy guy, and always used his credit card when paying for clothes, restaurant meals, and when they went out drinking. However, one day he suddenly stopped using his credit card. He started using cash to pay for everything. He also started going to less expensive places when they went out drinking. She thought it was a little strange.

"How come you're not using your credit card these days? What's going on? A change of heart?" She asked him this very casually, and he responded in an admirable way by saying, "I've been hearing about a lot of cases of people who fall into credit card hell, and have declared personal bankruptcy. I have to think of the future and start saving a little. I'm just trying to save money by going to cheaper places to drink. I hope you'll cooperate with me on this."

At first Rie believed him. But when she observed him carefully, she couldn't see any evidence that he was saving money, and she suspected something different.

Rie was frequently over at his apartment, so he knew that if she saw his itemized credit card statement she would be able to tell if he was seeing someone else.

He had his own car, but he was terrible at directions. Whenever they went for a drive, Rie always had to hold the map and do the navigating. One time, they were going somewhere they had never been before, but he was able to get there very smoothly without even looking at the map. When she said, "You seem to be pretty familiar with this area," he choked up for a moment and then answered that it was "animal instinct." Rie now had no doubt that he was cheating on her.

After that, when he took her to the beach one night, he had to ask her the directions over and over. So she said to him, "Your animal instincts don't seem to be working today. Is that because you haven't taken another woman here before?" He remained silent for awhile, and then said, "So you knew all along. I'm sorry."

He now uses his credit card only for Rie.

When a Woman Gets Caught Lying

For a woman, there is a very thin line between her pride and a lie. The two often go together, as one can see from the everyday conversations that go on between women. I've made a collection of the type of lies that women are prone towards telling to each other. Of course, they were presented to me as "not a lie that I've told" but "the kind of lie that my friends have told." It seems that women are very reluctant to talk about themselves honestly.

Lies about husbands and boyfriends
"My husband's family is really rich, so...." "My husband went to a really good college, so naturally we want the kids to..." "My boyfriend works in a really elite company, so he has to spend a lot of money entertaining," and even though her boyfriend is five years younger, "My boyfriend is three years younger than me" she says, lying about his age.

Lies told about oneself are easily found out. If you are lying to friends or neighbors, they probably already know all about you. However, lies about a husband or boyfriend won't be discovered unless somebody takes some kind of step to do so. So you can rest relatively easy when you tell them.

However, sometimes the jealousy of a woman can move her to do some stubborn investigation.

"My husband went to a really good college" was found to be a lie by a woman in the neighborhood who checked the alumnae listing for him and was unable to find his name. The lie that "my boyfriend works in a really elite company" was blown when the person who told it casually later said that they were going to get married, and she was having trouble budgeting since "his company gives no housing allowance." One of the friends she was bragging to had an acquaintance who worked at that company and when she asked them about it, they said that "our company does have a housing allowance." The truth was that he was working for a "subsidiary of an elite company."

Lies told to men

"You may think I look very flashy, but actually I'm really the kind who likes to cook and clean. I love cooking." "I've been studying flower arranging (she actually quit after three lessons)." "I've never been seriously involved with a man before."

When a woman lies to a man, she wants to be seen as a homey and earnest type, probably because this is what she assumes the man would want. When women's magazines have features on "the type of woman that I want to marry" it seems that the articles always turn out to be slanted towards the type of woman that the young editors themselves want.

Spur of the moment lies in the flow of conversation
"I'm planning a trip to Europe." "Well, I haven't told you about this yet, but I've had a really good proposal for an arranged marriage." "Well, you might not know it, but actually I only use the best brands, so I can't really use this one..."

Most of these kinds of lies are not deliberate ones. They happen during the natural flow of conversation. When a friend is talking about her plans to travel abroad, even though a woman has no plans of her own for a trip, she finds herself saying, "You know, I'm also..." to be included in the conversation. Among such women there are even those that have ended up taking trips that they don't really want to take so as to keep up with their friends. In the case of the lie about using only the "best brands" one woman told another, "I love Wedgwood dishes." The other woman then claimed, "I use them too." However, one day the two of them went shopping together. When the second woman looked at a dish that a true Wedgwood lover would automatically recognize, she said condescendingly that it had a strange pattern to it and consequently gave herself away.

A HOUSE'S APPEARANCE GIVES AWAY ITS OWNER

A saying from long ago tells us that "You can tell what is inside of a person's wallet by looking at their shoes." They say that among the clerks and inn keepers there were those that could take one look at the footwear of their guests and say exactly how much money they were carrying with them.

According to a floor model who has worked for many years at a high-class boutique, "Things are different today. You have to judge by their shoes, bag, and whether their whole 'look' is good."

In these times of prosperity, it seems that even if a customer is wearing expensive shoes, she may be exposed by wearing cheap accessories. The sales people know that they can't expect such a person to spend large amounts of money. They say that these days it is getting harder and harder to judge a person by their outward appearance.

Anybody can gloss over their wardrobe, but when it comes to one's home it is harder to hide the truth. Door-to-door salesmen all over the world are experts at observing carefully around the area of the house and judging what the outcome of their sales pitch will be. Among them are some salesmen running scams.

For example, there is the case of those salesmen who pretend to be firemen selling fire extinguishers. They say that when they go to a neighborhood they instinctively observe each of the houses they plan to visit.

The first thing that they take a look at is the entranceway and the laundry. They check to see if the lawn and shrubbery are neatly clipped, and whether the laundry is hung neatly or sloppily. If the laundry is not hung neatly then they surmise that the lady of the house has a loose personality and may be freer with spending money.

Next, they go around to the back of the house and check to see if there is a toilet fan or not. If there is a toilet fan installed then they go back around and knock on the door. The reason for this is that almost all toilet fans are sold by traveling salesmen. If someone has one it is like putting a sign up that says "this house is open to sales." Needless to say, these type of salesmen have a very high success rate.

There are some salesmen who boast that they can tell with one glimpse into the house whether or not the woman living there is the type they can get into bed. The front entranceway of the house is the area that the average housewife takes the most pride in, and if it is in a state of disarray, then they say that she is likely to be loose sexually as well and open to any invitation.

With that in mind, when you look at a residential street, you can see a great variety in the way houses look. The house itself radiates a certain atmosphere.

Corrupt sales practices are unforgivable. But this technique of observing houses may be a useful weapon for those door-to-door salesmen in competition to increase their sales, as well as for those trading in securities.

PEOPLE WHO FALL THE EASIEST FOR CORRUPT BUSINESS DEALS

This is yet another example of corrupt sales practices. This particular salesman has gotten his hands on large amounts of money from unsuspecting housewives who thought they were buying futures in rubber and coffee beans.

From his many years of experience he lists six types of people who are easy to fool.

1. People who are very interested in making money
2. People who have had bad experiences with banks or stock-brokerage firms
3. Cheerful people who enjoy talking with others
4. Naive people who are unsuspicious of others
5. Country people living in the city
6. Wives whose husbands are unfaithful and aren't happy at home

Looking over this list it is easy to see that these are the types of people who might fall for this kind of deal. He explains it as follows.

Type 1 people are greedy, making it easy to broach the subject with them. They know a lot about money making and are eager to join in on new ventures.

Only an amateur would join in with Type 2 people and start criticizing banks with them. Instead, he praises banks and stock-brokerage firms. When he does that, then the person speaks out even more strongly against banks. At that point only, he begins his talk about the disadvantages of banks. He keeps going until he has gotten their proxy to dissolve their bank accounts.

For Types 3 and 4, he engages them in talk for awhile and then brings out a newspaper article that supports what he is trying to do. These types have a complex about being well informed, and when shown this kind of information, they will then be very open to signing a contract with him.

For unsophisticated Type 5 people it is important to make them take leadership. "It is your job as a housewife to manage the household finances well." "You have to take the initiative," he says to bolster them. They gradually come to believe him.

Most of the Type 6 wives have secret savings squirreled away. "If you put this money into the bank, your husband is going to find out about it and take it away from you. You'd be smarter to put it into securities," he tells them. After that, he says to them that "even so, it is hard for someone who doesn't know the ropes to invest in stocks." He then continues with his recommendation of futures. In most cases they ask him to "keep it a secret from my husband."

It only takes this kind of corrupt salesmen a few seconds to size up his customer and choose the right technique. They speak in a friendly way to cheerful customers, and just keep up an idle conversation with more taciturn customers until the customers themselves start complaining. They have to be that fast at changing their techniques if they want to be successful at deceiving people.

PEOPLE FALL EASIEST FOR THE WILDEST SCHEMES

When I was a student I once went to a gathering of the UFO Society on my campus. Of course all of the members of the group believed in UFOs 100 percent.

I am naturally a very rational type (though all people who have been fooled will say this about themselves) and normally wouldn't believe in such a thing as a UFO. But on that day, as I listened to the "proof" that they gave of their existence, I remember that I became inclined to believe 90 percent of what they were saying. All of the members were very fervent as they talked about objects that came flying from unknown places. They talked about where they had come from and who had had contact with people from outer space....

However, if I think about it now, what almost made me a believer was not the feeling that their proof was credible, but rather the way that they spoke so convincingly, with such infectious zeal. Their enthusiasm seemed to penetrate my doubt.

Actually, when a human heart is penetrated, you become careless and open to believing anything. No matter how strange of a thing it may be, you will easily believe. In fact, the wilder it seems, the easier it may be to believe!

Why is it that the wildest things are the easiest to believe? I can explain that by explaining the mechanism of the heart.

First of all, let's consider the movie world. Films from simple literary works do not set the world on fire. The big hits are always action movies or romances or splashy science fiction movies. The almost inhuman actions of Sylvester Stallone and Arnold Schwarznegger are things that couldn't be found in real life, but young people applaud them. And in real life it almost never happens that two people's eyes meet and they fall totally in love. Even so, people believe it when it happens on screen.

People enjoy these films because they are bored

with their own everyday lives. People go to the movies to escape and become absorbed in the places and scenarios that never happen to them in real life. But as long as they are inside the darkness of the movie theater, they don't have to worry about anything else.

The desire to escape from one's life is a common one for many people. That is exactly why there are so many people who will believe in something like a UFO, though there is absolutely no scientific proof of their evidence. If science were to come up with an explanation for flying saucers' existence, then probably not very many people would believe in them. The UFO Society that I mentioned previously has an annual meeting where they claim to call in flying saucers. They say that at that meeting, several hundreds of flying saucers appear in the skies above.

And the strangest thing of all is that even though not one member of the society has ever seen them, all of them believe in their existence. If I now tell you that this UFO Society is made up of Tokyo University students then probably all of you will be even more surprised! [12]

---

[12] Tokyo University is the top university in Japan. It could be equated to Harvard University in America, and most people assume that students there are very serious and intellectual.

LIFE IS MADE UP OF LIES

Just as I have been explaining, we live in a world made of lies. "Earnestness" and "honesty" are really lies.

Just as I have said, the ability to tell a lie well is the secret to life. But is it possible that a world exists where truth reigns? Now I would like to tell you about a very unusual case that I myself experienced.

Etsuko is currently the founder of a new religious sect that has many believers. After she graduated from a local college, she found employment at a day care center. At that time, she began to hear strange voices, or the "voice of God," as she put it, in her head. Following the voice's instructions, she ran out of her house at night and started visiting all of the neighboring homes, knocking on their doors.

The voices in her head were telling her that "in order for you to become the savior for all of these people you must do such and such." So, in order to save people, she began knocking on doors of strangers to chase away spirits. Both good and bad spirits invaded her body, and since it was very difficult for her to exorcise the bad spirits she kept forcing herself to go on as part of her own ascetic training. From a psychiatric point of view, she was suffering from strong auditory hallucinations as well as delusional hallucinations which caused her to take these strong actions.

After three months of hospitalization in a mental hospital, she returned to her job as a public employee and eventually married and gave birth to three children. But at the birth of her eldest son, due to a mistake in administering anesthesia, she lay in a near-death state for seven hours. During that time, she had a very special vision and says that she reached an awareness of her reason for living.

Etsuko's encounter with other planet's beings, specifically Venusians, goes back to when she was in elementary school. According to her, she was already having contact with Venusians back then, and not just in her dreams either. She says that she met with them in the fields, but kept it bottled up inside of her and continued on with life. Often, there is a fine line between reality and our imagination, and perhaps what Etsuko saw was only a daydream. But for our purposes it is not productive to consider that interpretation here.

After Etsuko gave birth to her eldest son, she felt she had reached enlightenment and began to get involved with a variety of religious activities. One of the movements she became involved with was therapy for troubled children. A pyramid was placed in the middle of a large room. She would then put a purifying rock that she had received from a Venusian on top of the pyramid. The children would form a circle around it and sit down and meditate. When she did this, most of the children would fall into a trance and have their spirit "purified."

Her activities became well known among the people around them. Believers started to naturally congregate and a new religious sect was born. Etsuko said to them that "ninety percent of me is God, and ten percent of me is a housewife." The number of believers continued to increase.

The mix of the Japanese style of living God with the predictions coming from Venusians, along with the pyramid power, was very eclectic from a religious standpoint. But when I actually visited her I had no impression of any artificiality or unnaturalness whatsoever. This founder of a small new religion had what could be called a hysterical personality and some eccentricity, but she spoke very straightforwardly about her past experiences. Even I could feel some radiance in her impeccable personality.

Etsuko's case seems similar to the other examples of communication with people from different planets. But what is different is that she does not put any emphasis on UFOs. Her life in a local mental hospital was probably a big shock to her. But she put that experience behind her and went back to normal life and goes on speaking the truth.

I do not know any other examples where the

"truth" has been successful. Etsuko was protected and saved, and then went on to save others. According to Etsuko there are thousands of people from other planets. And I cannot completely prove she's not telling the truth.

Chapter 7
LIES KEEP OUR SOCIETY GOING

STATISTICS AND OPINION POLLS

In our modern society, statistics created from opinion or other kinds of polls are looked upon as a kind of magic. Although they are extremely effective tools in convincing people of something, the actual scientific basis for the numbers is very vague. It is very easy to manipulate statistics into saying what you want them to say.

These days, not only the mass media but businessmen as well are apt to make full use of statistics. Here too the basis for the statistics is close to being fraudulent. If we examine the reasons why we use statistical data to back up what we are trying to talk about, it is easier to understand.

When a person looks at a list of plausible numbers all lined up they tend to believe what is being told to them. Furthermore, if they are told that the numbers represent "the results of a survey given to a large number of people," then they will not look very carefully at the content of the questions that were asked and will instead accept the results uncritically. Perhaps statistics have magical powers, similar to those involved in brainwashing. If you don't want to be fooled by statistics, you must first look at who it is that has put the statistics together and with what intention.

One historically famous example of statistics gone wrong is the 1936 reelection of the American President Franklin Delano Roosevelt.

At this time, a certain magazine conducted an opinion poll. The results predicted that Roosevelt, the Democratic Party candidate, would suffer a crushing defeat, and that the opposing Republican candidate would have an overwhelming victory. However, at the actual election Roosevelt was the victor by a wide margin. The reason for the wrong prediction lay in the method of polling. The sampling of people used for the poll was biased in one direction, toward Republican voters.

Since the names for this huge opinion poll were taken out of the white pages of the phone book and from lists of home owners, the people polled were all from an affluent class (most of whom did not support Roosevelt).

I should add that at this time the scientific random sampling method which had just been established by the statician Gallup accurately predicted the results of the election and caused a kind of revolution in the standards for opinion polls at the time.

Compared to those times, the methods currently used for opinion polls are much more sophisticated. The up-to-the-minute news flashes that we see during elections are done by using just one percent of the ballots counted, and "sure victory" marks are placed accordingly. These results are the product of the results of prior opinion polls and the state of ballot counting, but miscalculations are still possible. At a previous election for the House of Representatives, a number of television stations put a "sure victory" mark on a certain candidate who ultimately failed to win a seat, showing that we cannot always trust the results of these statistics.

If someone is trying to convince you of something through the use of statistics, examine the statistics themselves. Look at what intention they were made for. Is the sampling really appropriate to the question? Are the questions themselves biased so as to elicit a certain answer? All of these things influence the results.

LOSING YOUR POWER OF JUDGMENT

Brainwashing was originally developed as a method of infusing a certain kind of political thought, such as Communism, into individuals. Today it has come to be used not only in political thought, but more widely in religion and even in corrupt business practices. When someone wants to brainwash a certain person or group, they usually work under the following conditions.

First of all, they shut the person up in an enclosed space and give them only enough food and water to stay alive. Sleeping hours are minimal. Often light is shut out, so they lose the distinction between night and day. Through all this, the power of judgment is affected, and at times they suffer from hallucinations and other mental abnormalities.

When they have reached a totally exhausted state, and stimulus from the outside world is ceased, human beings fall into a state of confusion. Their mental foundation is completely destroyed. When they find someone who ingratiates themselves to them and is willing to accept them, they cling to them and accept what they say without criticism.

The fundamental plan for this is something like "destruction of self → the appearance of something that will protect me." This is the point where it is possible to introduce certain thoughts, dogma, or multi-level marketing schemes.

When they are successful, and a reward is made for success, the effects of brainwashing are reinforced even more. Multi-level marketing systems rely on this heavily as do religious groups. Groups such as the Aum Shinri-Kyo[13] give members higher levels of rank as they progress in their faith.

Brainwashing is often done on groups. Not is it faster than working on individuals one by one, it is easier to carry out brainwashing as a group.

It isn't necessary to have an entire group in such an extreme state as mentioned previously. Sleeping time and amounts of food are cut down on slightly so that the members are feeling some exhaustion or fatigue. During discussion time they are encouraged to point out each other's faults. Just by doing this, a person's concept of themselves can easily be destroyed. At this time, if a leader evolves from the group and states a new opinion, most of the people are prepared to accept it.

Human beings will not readily give up their fundamental beliefs without a good reason. However, under these special circumstances, they will often quite simply change their minds.

A few years ago, pyramid schemes, so-called endless chain sales, were popular among university students. When new members were canvassed, one person was targeted and then four or five of them would gather to hear an explanation. Most of the sales pitches were done at night at the lodgings or small apartments of the students in a tiny room.

---

[13]A cult which gained worldwide notoriety through their use of sarin in subway bombings.

The talks would go on for hours about the benefits of participation. If the students being targeted said, "I want to go home and think about it," they would ask that the pitch be stopped there since the headquarters had told them to do it like that. They knew from experience that this was the way to brainwash.

If a person was left alone to think, rather than staying with others, they would be able to think calmly and rationally. Most of the students would likely not want to participate. So they would use a kind of gentle threat, saying, "Well, then let's just forget the whole thing." They would pressure the student to decide right then and there whether or not he wanted to participate.

This kind of method is common to all types of "brainwashing." The Nazi Germany speeches given by Hitler were almost all done at dusk in an area where tens of thousands of people were gathered. They were made to stand for hours, until they were exhausted. Plants sprinkled through the crowd would begin to call out "Heil Hitler" and arouse the crowd.

Losing their power of judgment, people fell into the illusion that they spoke of their own free will, and they too began to shout out "Heil Hitler!" This kind of illusion spread out of the city centers and throughout the country. It was such an enormous swelling, it soon shook world history as well.

If brainwashing is successful, a person can be coerced into believing any kind of lie.

GULLIBLE PEOPLE GET FOOLED OVER AND OVER AGAIN

There are many groups, such as the Aum Religious Sect, that have been accused of doing "group brainwashing" by the mass media. This is a report from a woman who used to be a member of such a group; in fact, she was in charge of educating new members to the group.

The group all lived collectively in a kind of dorm together, but before a new member could move in there, he or she was investigated to find out whether or not they had any savings or loans to pay off. If they had savings, their acceptance into the group was instantly approved, and if they had debts to pay off they were told to work another job and pay them off before they would be allowed to live with the group.

However, this woman found that when she investigated the members, who were around twenty years of age, almost all of them had debts. This surprised her. Furthermore, the kind of debt was very similar in all cases.

Most of the men had been fooled by "date" sales methods and had ended up buying cassette tapes for learning English conversation, costing them up to several thousand dollars. Just like the name implies, a young woman would call them and invite them out. When they went to meet her, she would end up selling them a huge amount of English language materials and lessons.

The women of the group had been taken in by "boyfriend" sales methods and been talked into buying expensive kimonos. This method is a little more insidious than the above "date" sales method. A man would call them up and they would begin dating. After some time, she would be forced into buying an expensive kimono. Most of the women thought that "if I don't buy it, he won't ask me out anymore" and would end up spending the money.

Gullible people get fooled over and over again.....

I want to add one thing. I personally respect those new religions that are truly authentic. I know that many include members who are sincerely walking the path of faith. However, it is also a fact that there are groups that should be completely steered clear of. These are groups that destroy a person's character. The group that this woman belonged to was of this type.

People who are easily fooled by "date" or "boyfriend" sales methods are also easily brainwashed by religious groups. This is because they have grown up with fewer defenses in their psychological makeup, and are too trusting towards strangers. On top of all that, they also have little experience in examining objectively their relationships with others in society.

People like this are very easily fooled. If you think that you may have a little of this in yourself as well, then chances are you'll be okay. It is the people who think to themselves, "I'd never be tricked like that" who are the most susceptible.

LIES TO HELP A CHILD GET BETTER GRADES

I heard something interesting recently from an elementary school teacher.

When a teacher works with children they are supposed to be impartial. However, teachers are human beings as well, and can't help having certain preconceptions about their students.

"This child gets very good grades so I'm sure she will do well the second semester as well." Or, "This child just can't seem to settle down, so I'm sure that his grades will get worse."

Strangely enough, these preconceptions end up being correct most of the time.

Some of this is due to the fact that an experienced teacher can accurately predict these things. But it is also undeniable that a teacher's preconceptions and prejudices shape the behavior of the child. As this man said, "A child becomes what he is expected to become." There are many cases in which this has already been proved.

A certain psychologist did an experiment at an elementary school on this. A child with just average grades was appointed class representative by the teacher. When this happened, the grades of this child went up during the next semester and he was ranked at the top of the class. The child thought to himself that "my teacher has expectations for me" and put much greater effort into his study.

Even a person who has no particular talent and doesn't stand out at all will gain confidence when praised by another person, and their ability will improve in all facets. This is a kind of natural law.

Sometimes even an elementary school student who gets bad grades in everything will show improvement in all subject areas when praised in one subject. So if you want your child to get better grades, rather than scolding him, it would be more effective to praise him lavishly in the area that he excels at, such as science or art.

Especially in drawing, if you praise even a poorly done picture, that child's drawings will become better and better. In this case, it is said that not only praising, but giving a higher grade rather than the lower one deserved, is effective.

This does not only apply to children. If you praise the strong points of an adult woman or man she or he will gradually become confident and effective. And the same can be said for managers and employees.

DUAL AND MULTIPLE PERSONALITIES

There are many kinds of lies that you can tell about or to yourself. What if you were to try to deny the sexual desire that every one of us possesses? What would happen if you were to try to drive its existence from your heart?

The sexual drive, with very few and rare exceptions, is a basic human drive that exists in us all. It is only in the last one or two thousand years, through the influence of human morality, that it has been thought of as something impure or dirty. When in fear of this thin veil of morality, a person will act as if he or she has no sexual desire, and will try to repress their urges.

There was once a very uptight woman in America named Sally. She was a modest woman who stood by her husband and devoted herself to bringing up their children. Of course, she was never one to speak in a loud voice, or bring up the subject of sex, and was a very quiet and conservative woman.

But since she was unable to display her sexuality, she felt very dissatisfied. On the surface she showed nothing at all, but in fact she had strong sexual urges that were buried beneath the surface of her personality.

She went on living her usual life, until one day Sally became Susan. Her personality split in two and the two personalities came to live in her one body. This is what we call a "dual personality."

Compared to the very chaste Sally, Susan was very coquettish. She wasn't embarrassed about her sex appeal and the attention she drew from men. The interesting thing about this case was that while Susan was aware of Sally's existence, Sally knew nothing of Susan's existence. She had no idea that her other self was going out on the town prowling around in search of men. However, Susan knew that there was another person inside of her named Sally who was very modest. This is very typical of dual personalities.

Was Susan or Sally the real personality of this woman?

From a social point of view, the answer would be Sally. From a medical standpoint, Susan was the sub-personality who was just a mirror of Sally. However, from the point of view of the woman's consciousness herself, I believe that she might say that Susan was actually the real her.

Sub-personalities are not just found in dual personalities, but also appear during psychic trances. There are some psychiatrists who believe that all of us have sub-personalities in us somewhere that are being repressed in our daily lives. But when a sub-personality appears continuously, it is usually due to the constant suppression of some hope or desire on the part of the person.

Lying to yourself about your desires, if done skillfully, can be a way to reform yourself and turn the tides of fate. But it is possible to shift off in the wrong direction, and you should be aware of the fact that this kind of psychological damage can occur.

There is also another aspect to multiple personalities, which is that society itself builds multiple personalities. In America during the period between 1950 and 1960 many cases of multiple personalities caught the eye of the public. Since then, the phenomena has ceased to be all that unusual. In Japan there have been hardly any cases of actual multiple personalities. The defendant in the case of the serial killings of young girls has been diagnosed as having multiple personalities. This may result in an increase in appearances of the phenomena here as well.

THE TRUTH AND LIES OF PSYCHOLOGICAL ASSESSMENT

The following experiment was once done in America. Ten adult men went to psychiatrists complaining that they heard voices in their head. The purpose of the experiment was to see in what way they would be diagnosed based merely on that one symptom.

Hearing voices in your head is a symptom known as auditory hallucination, but with just this symptom alone it is impossible to give the diagnosis of schizophrenia. However, almost all of the doctors of these ten healthy men diagnosed the problem as schizophrenia and attempted to start treatment along those lines.

If these patients had gone to a different type of doctor, rather than a psychiatrist, they may not have automatically assumed a mental illness. Specialists see mental patients everyday and assume automatically that the patients are not telling lies. They listen to the symptoms and give their diagnosis.

From experience, they can say that if somebody complains of auditory hallucinations, if they are not drunk, and if they are between the ages of 20 and 30, then the chance of schizophrenia is extremely high, but auditory hallucinations just on their own do not form the basis for a diagnosis of schizophrenia. Yet almost all of the ten doctors quickly came up with this mistaken diagnosis. Nobody is as easy to fool as a specialist. That lie caused a wrong diagnosis and as a result made them guilty of grave errors.

How does this affect psychological assessment?

Psychological assessment is done on those persons who have committed a serious crime and have a past record of mental illness. Due to the grave nature of this assessment, a large number of specialists are consulted and careful psychological testing of the person is done. The details of his or her mental state before and after the crime are carefully considered. On top of that, the current mental state is closely examined and a final assessment is drawn up.

In spite of this rigorous process, the assessment of one defendant often ends up with completely different results from different examiners.

The psychological assessment of Defendant M currently on trial for serial murders of young girls was an exception. The specialists worked together on the initial assessment. Knowing that the eyes of the public were upon them, the first assessment team took nearly one year to produce a document over 500 pages long for the court. The results claimed that there was no sign of any mental illness and the conclusion was that the defendant bore full responsibility for his actions.

After that, the lawyers demanded that he be assessed again, and three psychiatrists carried out the assessment separately. This time two totally different assessment results were made. One of them diagnosed the defendant as "schizophrenic," with limited responsibility for his actions, and the other said that he suffered from "multiple personality disorder" and agreed his responsibility was limited. Most of the other specialists were particularly surprised by the diagnosis of multiple personality disorder, and though they did not object, were very suspicious of the results.

The term "feigned illness" is used to describe a person who fakes an illness to their doctor. If a person has some skill for acting, it isn't hard to fake a multiple personality disorder to a doctor.

In a recent murder case in America one defendant claimed, "I didn't do it. Another personality inside of me used my hands and committed this crime." He also said that this other personality came out and gave a new name as the person who did it. Afterwards they found that a person of that name really did exist, and the criminal knew that person's name and used it. He then claimed that "the other personality gave you that name, not me." And in truth the court was amazed by the brazenness of the act.

In Japan, too, the introduction of the multiple personalities disorder into the courtroom will cause confusion. I myself do not entirely believe that Defendant M is faking it, but I also can't deny the possibility that the doctors themselves have induced the multiple personality disorder.

If multiple personalities exist, to which personality should questions be addressed in a court trial?

This is only the first problem. In America a person is sworn in before they are allowed to testify in court. In this case, if a person had seven different personalities, must they all be sworn in separately? And, even more strangely, if one of the personalities should happen to be a dog or other animal, should we swear them in as well? Clearly the testimony of a person with multiple personalities disorder is very problematic in court.

It would be a lie to say that persons with multiple personalities have a higher crime rate than the general population. (Their crime rate is actually lower.) However, the rate of serious crimes, such as arson, is higher for persons with multiple personalities.

The more carefully a diagnosis by a specialist is carried out, the more unconsciously the assessor will tend to go with the initial prediction. Why is that so? The more skillful the specialist, the more confidence he has in his diagnostic abilities and understanding of many academic theories. His opinions are stronger than a more general clinical doctor.

Observation is the basis for almost all of science, but to "read" the state of the heart requires an interpretation.

No such clinical reading can be entirely objective. One's own background, a huge amount of learned academic knowledge, and the predjudices of a specialist towards a certain grave incident are already influencing the reading of the symptoms, which are the basis for the diagnosis. No matter how well trained a specialist is, it's hard to come to any case without judgment.

What All Con Artists Know About

In looking at the crimes that con artists commit, one often wonders how it is that people can fall for what seems like such obvious lies. It is hard to know if it is because the swindlers are so clever, or because the swindlees are so stupid. Here are some examples of swindles that have been successful over that last few years.

- Claiming to represent a top wedding dress designer, a man recruited young women asking them, "Wouldn't you like to be a fashion model?" He robbed them of an "agent's fee" of a few thousand dollars each. Twenty young women were fooled out of tens of thousands of dollars.

- A newspaper ad claimed that you could get tickets to the American superstar Michael Jackson's Kansai Tour, and collected $250 a person. They didn't get into the concert. The number of persons falling victim to this scheme is unknown.

- A man claimed to represent a restaurant guide and had restaurant owners pay $400 each to be included in it. Victims were located nationwide and 517 restaurants fell for this scheme, a total of $200,000 for this man. The man carried a notebook and a camera with him and claimed to represent a certain publishing company.

- "If you will buy a vending machine for women's underwear, our company will install and maintain it for you. Cash isn't necessary because all costs above those of the loan payments will be paid from the profits." Victims of this scheme were talked into taking out loans by this man. The machines cost $14,000 each and actually did exist, but of course they were never installed. Forty people fell for this scheme and their losses came to a total of over $500,000.

- "If you take out a loan for us, we'll give you half of it. The payments will be done by another company so you don't have to worry about it." This man targeted members of the Marine Self Defense Force and tricked twenty persons out of $400,000. When this man was apprehended, he told police that "it is easy to trick members of the Self Defense Force, because most of them are such simpletons."

- Using the imitation gold nuggets sold for $25 each at the AmeYoko Arcade in Ueno one man was able to trick metal dealers out of $100,000. The "gold nuggets" were really just lead, and even though they were labeled in English as "imitation," this man had the nuggets wrapped in tissue paper and told them some ridiculous story about how they "couldn't be unwrapped without a witness."

• One man pretending to be a school administrator called a student's home. "Your child has shoplifted an expensive watch and then destroyed it. I'd like to keep this from leaking out, so please bring me the money to pay for it." He was able to trick seven people out of $14,000 this way. He explained that he had appealed to the hearts of the parents and said that if he told the parents that their child had been forced into this behavior by an upperclassman, it was quite easy to deceive the parents.

• Another man approached the carpentry shop which had run an ad in the paper searching for carpenters. He offered to introduce them to some carpenters for a fee. He tricked 30 businesses this way out of $100,000. These businesses suffer chronic shortages of manpower and are desperate to find workers, since if they fail to complete a job on time, they must pay compensatory fees. He says that he was never once doubted by these companies, whose need he had cleverly hit upon.

• "I'm from the Tax Administration Agency. We've

found some discrepancies in your returns so I've come here to take a look at your records." Two men said these words to the director of a hospital and went into his study. They "seized" his savings account passbook and made him send an employee to the bank to withdraw the funds. They got $100,000 this way. They picked out small hospitals where there had probably been some creative accounting, and the two men spent four hours in the study pretending to be employees of the Tax Administration Agency.

Looking at these cases, we could almost believe that the world is made up of only two types of human beings—those who are easily fooled and those who easily fool.

LIES BECOME THE TRUTH IN MOB PSYCHOLOGY

No matter how cool and rational a person may be, when they become part of a large crowd, they lose their rationality and are more easily swayed by lies. The most extreme examples of this are the false rumors that abound during times of natural disasters.

Some years ago in South America during a major earthquake the rumor spread that "there is an elementary school age boy singing songs from beneath the rubble of a fallen building." The rescue workers

tore away at the mountain of cement and continued to frantically search for the boy. But in the end,
neither the boy nor any body emerged from the
rubble. This rumor was just the kind that came
about from the discouraged people wanting some
kind of hope.

Mob mentality comes about when a large number of people are gathered in one place and feel
some sense of unity. Rumors fly easiest when the
unifying factor is an unorganized one, rather than
an organized one. Being victims in the same boat of
a natural disaster is very consistent with this.

There are several characteristics of mob mentality, but the most representative ones are the
easy acceptance of rumors as truth, being very
open to suggestion, having little or no sense of individual responsibility, and tending to act impul-
sively. In this case it would be almost unheard of
for one person's rational sense of judgment to influence all of them.

In these cases, the group is like some living creature with a huge shared consciousness that is liable
to take off in any direction. If one lonely member of
the group tried to make the rest of the group remain
calm and objective, that member would likely be
put down.

During the 1989 San Francisco Earthquake,
there were no reports of any great panic or rumors.
They say that this is because most of the people had

their ears tuned to transistor radios where they were able to get accurate reports on the earthquake. In this case the consciousness of the people who had a possibility of becoming a group remained separate and rational, thanks to the facts on the radio. They were able to maintain their individual composure and sense of judgment. Sometimes the media, which is often criticized for heralding sensational information, has a beneficial role in society as well.

During the Great Hanshin Earthquake, it is said that there were no rumors nor persecution against certain types of people, at least at first. All of the people cooperated with each other and had a strong feeling of solidarity as they lived in evacuation centers together. But as time passed, different kinds of reports began to circulate. A soothsayer predicted that on a certain date a major earthquake would strike the Tokyo area. Even though many of these predictions proved to be false, nobody was able to ignore them as new ones came out. Uneasiness and rumors abounded, making it difficult to maintain good judgment and ignore mistaken reports.

Mass media reports themselves are only the products of ordinary people who form a group. The reality that we as an audience are presented with is what the media has created for us.

When a "psychic" is recognized by a TV station, then the station is overwhelmed by requests asking for introductions. However, in reality, the TV station's staff may have invented the psychic and even told the psychic how to speak and what mannerisms to use to impress people.

The truth presented to us by a television station is often just made up. Television is truly a treasury of lies.

Chapter 8
How to Lie Well—
Lies That Work and
Some That don't

Lies That Women Tell

Lies about time

• **Fake messages**

"I'm sorry. Have you been waiting long? I was running behind, so I left a message on your answering machine that I'd be about 30 minutes late. What?! It wasn't on there? My gosh, so you've been waiting 40 minutes?!"

—Machines aren't perfect, so telling a lie that you left a message on his machine works every time.

• **The reason for being late**

"I'm so sorry. Just as I was ready to walk out the door I got a phone call from my mother that my father was really sick and I should come home immediately. Of course I tried calling you at home right away, but you'd already left...."

—Lies about a parent's "illness" are pretty old

hat, but still work well. Watch out for divine retribution, though.

"I was about to leave when my boss came in and said, "I really need this done in a hurry." It wasn't anything complicated so I knew I could get it done quickly, but I guess it took longer than I thought. I'm really sorry."

—When you use "work" as an excuse for being late, be careful not to do it too often. Even a really patient guy will suspect that you're having an affair.

"What do you mean, why didn't I show up today? You've got to be kidding. We were supposed to get together yesterday. I waited over two hours for you in our usual place!"

—When you make a strong counterattack using a "threatening" lie you have to pull out all the stops and be a total "wicked woman."

HUSBAND: "You're awfully late. It's one in the morning, for God's sake."

WIFE: "Well, what time did you get home?"

HUSBAND: "After 11! Just because you had a class reunion doesn't mean that you can come back so late. What were you doing anyway? "

WIFE: "Three of us went over to Haruko's place after the reunion. I knew I'd get home late, so I tried calling you at 9 and then at 10:30!"

—By finding out first of all what time her husband had returned home she could then claim to have called. She was very skilled with this "alibi method."

Say It Without Saying It
• **To the one you love**
"My friends all say that when you're not around, I have no sparkle to me at all. They're telling me that I should 'hurry up and get married.'"

"Narumi says that if a guy really likes you, he wants to get you in bed. She says that if he isn't trying to do that, he isn't attracted to you. Aren't you attracted to me?"

—If you have trouble bringing up certain topics then it may be easier to bring them up by saying "somebody said that...."

"These days when we part and it's time to head for home, the way back always seem to be so long. I wonder when we'll be able to live together?"

—Rather than saying that you love him or that you want to get married, it is better to say it indirectly. This kind of feminine wile works better on men than on women.

• **When you want to make up**
"I was really really tired then. I don't even remember what I said. I may have said something really cruel, but I didn't mean it at all. Please forgive me."

"I'm no good without you. All I can do is think about you all day long. Remember that fight we had? Well, now I know how much I need you."

Telephone lies

• **When you want to check if someone is home or not**

"It's nothing. I just wanted to hear your voice. I'm really sorry to call so late at night."

• **When you need to get off quickly**

"I was just about to walk out the door...."

"Whoops, somebody's ringing the doorbell. Sorry, we'll talk later."

"Oh my God, I forgot about the fish I was grilling!"

• **To late night callers**

"I'm sorry. I have to get up really early tomorrow morning."

(To a woman friend) "Well, actually, my boyfriend is spending the night so...."

"Lately I have been getting crank calls late at night so I've stopped answering the phone at this hour. So, don't call me this late any more, okay?"

—A precaution like this is necessary in advance for people who call late and disturb your sleep.

• **Answering machines**

"Mai, your answering machine was on all day yesterday. Where were you?"

(Actually she was on a date with another boyfriend.)

"Yeah. I left it on because I was out all day with my friend Kaori shopping in Yokohama."

"Come on, pick up the phone. You're there aren't you?"

—One of her friends who knew she was intentionally using the answering machine, even though she was at home, left this message on the phone.

At a night club
- **A hostess speaking to a male customer**

"If you let me fall for you then I'll do anything for you. Really. There aren't many women like me that are willing to do anything for a man. That's what everyone says about me."

"It's like some kind of dream that you said to me, 'Junko, I'm going to buy you your own condominium someday.' I'm so stupid that I believed you. But I'd rather have you than a condominium."

"I know I said I'd go to a hotel with you. But I meant for dinner.... I never said I'd spend the night with you there. Isn't it a little early yet for that?"

—Getting a man in the mood and then at the last minute changing your mind is a clever move.

"I've been waiting and waiting thinking that surely today would be the day that you would show up. But every time I see you, I feel sad the next morning. Today I looked so depressed that I was scolded by my boss."

—In the world of the night there are those words which sound good to a man who has had a few drinks. But the man, too, must deliberately be "foolish" or "kind" enough to go along with these lies.

Lies to make invitations

"My friends Seiko and Misaki keep asking me, 'Haven't you gone to bed with him yet?'"

"I just really don't feel like going home alone tonight. I want to go out and drink some more. Please take me anywhere you want to."

—When a woman is the one doing the inviting, naturally the invitation must be made more subtly.

"My husband has been cheating on me...we even sleep in separate rooms. I promise I won't hold you responsible for anything we do...."

"I haven't slept with my husband in over six months. My husband is a workaholic and is completely stressed out. So he hasn't been able to....you know? And then I found out that he had a girlfriend. He was doing it with her twice a week! When I think about that I feel like I'm going to go crazy..."

—If you are going to fool around, then be sure that the man that you are fooling around with has the lightest burden possible. This way just about any man can be seduced.

Lies in bed

• **If you are both single**

"Tonight is our special night. For a woman there is never a night like this again..... I'm glad that you are the first one for me....Actually I was really scared about this before."

—If the man is the type who wants you to be a

virgin, then afterwards it is important to do some quick thinking.

• **To someone you are fooling around with**
"That was really great. Really. I've never been so satisfied before. My husband has never been all that good for me and I've been left feeling unsatisfied for a long time..."

"My doctor says that I'll never get pregnant. So we don't have to use anything..."

"I really want to have your baby. I'll raise it by myself, you won't have to do a thing."

—It is best to hide your calculated moves as a woman behind words which play up to a man.

• **To a husband who fizzled out**
"You're tired from all that nonsense you have to deal with at work. When you get that taken care of, I know you'll be fine again."

"It doesn't matter if this happens once or twice. No problem. Don't worry about me because it doesn't bother me one bit. You just get some rest."

—Even if your words are not true, what is important is not to overdo it. If you use words like "feel better" or "don't worry" then you can save your husband from low self-esteem.

Lies when drinking
"I don't remember anything from that night. Did I say anything strange? I hope you didn't take anything I said seriously. I was really drunk."

"All of a sudden I felt so drunk. I don't remember anything at all. I didn't mean to hurt your feelings. It is all because I got drunk..."

—A man can't get away with this kind of excuse, but most women can.

"I feel safe with you so I can go ahead and drink all I want. It looks like I've gotten really drunk. I wonder if I can get home okay on my own...."

—When she says "I'm really drunk" in almost all cases a woman is really not that drunk.

Lies to say no

• **To say no to a relationship**

"I'm really sorry. I wish I had gotten to know you sooner. I didn't want to tell you this, but actually there is a guy that I am involved with!"

• **To turn down an omiai**

"These days I just live for my job. I don't want to stop working to get married. Besides, I don't think that I would make a very submissive wife. No house should have two masters!"

• **A proposition from a superior at work**

"That kind of invitation isn't like you at all. I'd rather think of you as a really sweet older man."

—When a young woman says to a man that "that isn't like you at all" and calls him an "older man" the man is made aware of his age and in most cases won't pursue it any further.

"Your invitation makes me really happy! But it wouldn't be fair to my boyfriend and if he were to find out...I could never guess what he might do..."

—Even if you don't have this kind of "ferocious boyfriend" you can still hint at it.

"I hear that your wife is really pretty...I'd love to meet her."

- **Turning down an invitation to bed**

"I'm sorry. It isn't 'safe' today."

"I don't have a change of clothes or any 'protection' with me.... And these days when I spend the night out my mother asks too many questions. So tonight I really can't...."

"These days I'm so low on sleep that I can't concentrate on anything. I'm really sorry but I just don't want to tonight."

"If we start that kind of relationship it will be over quickly. I'd rather keep things the same and value our friendship...."

—Don't just react with a "NO!" when you turn a man down. Put a little thought into it.

Lies for breaking up

- **With a man you've been with for a long time**

"You're way too good for me... I'm the one who is no good. I've tried my best, but I just can't do it..."

"We've just been fooling each other up till now.

At least I know I have. If we keep going like this we'll both suffer, so let's just go our separate ways..."

• To a younger man

"I still love you. But even if we get married I won't be a good wife. You need to find someone much younger than I am. I know a man like you will find someone better than me quickly."

"There is nothing wrong with you. I just want to get to know some different people and widen my horizons. I guess I'm just a little selfish."

—If the woman is the one breaking up, and if she claims to be in the wrong, then she can do it without injuring the man's pride.

• To a man you were never really serious about

"I'm sorry it didn't work out between us in the end, but if I am ever born again then I'd want to be with you."

"If we keep going on like this, I'll feel torn apart. I want to keep all of my memories with you good. Right now the good memories are still stronger..."

—No matter who you are parting with, there is a desire for a "romantic parting." So it is good to prepare your words in advance.

• When someone wants to break up with you

"Do you mean that I'm 'too good' for you?"

"What? Do you really think that? There isn't anyone else that is going to love you like I do."

—It is at these times in particular that you want

to come back with a clever retort. You want to at least keep your pride as a woman.

• When an old boyfriend gets married

"At last I feel like I've graduated from being a beginner at love!"

"Well, now you and I can have a really good relationship as friends."

—You may not really mean it, but the workings of a woman's heart are complex.

Lies with tears

"Megumi, I know you've been with another guy. Why are you lying to me? Come on, say something."

MEGUMI: (tears).

—No matter what he says to you, just keep looking at the ground and crying. In the end, the man will be left with nothing to say and give up. The tears of a woman can pierce the heart of a caring man.

Saying nothing

"Why didn't you answer the door? I know you were in your room. You had a man there with you, didn't you?"

Woman "......"

"Come on. Say something!"

—This is closely related to lies with tears. When you are in danger of being caught in a lie, or when you find yourself at a disadvantage, switch to the tactic of silence.

Lies of laughter

"You're accusing me of taking a trip with another guy? I've never heard of anything more ridiculous in my life. Why don't you call my friend Emiko, whom you've met, and ask her about it? The two of us were in Hokkaido together traveling around...I wonder what reaction Emiko will have when you call her? Ha ha ha."

—There are many different meanings in laughter, but often a bold lie is hidden by a laugh.

Lying about your age

"Well, you know, all women lie about their age and take off about 4 or 5 years. I don't like to do that kind of thing, so I am very honest about being 39."

—In spite of these words, she is actually three years older.

"My age? Well, how old do I look?"

"Hmmm. About 25 or 26 I guess.... Yeah, 25."

"You guessed right!" (She is really 29.)

—If the person guesses a number younger than you are, immediately agree.

Finding out your partner's feelings

"It looks like I'm pregnant...."

"What? Are you sure? Boy, that is a problem. I guess there is nothing for you to do but to get an abortion."

"How can you say that so easily? You probably never really cared for me...."

"I do, but that is a different matter."

"That is quite all right. I just made it up anyway. I just wanted to see what you would say."

—If you tell a really exaggerated lie like this, it is important to get the timing right when you reveal that it was a lie after all.

• **To a man who you want more attention from**

"My parents back home have an omiai set up for me. I guess I'll go along with it and meet the guy. What do you think?"

"I guess that you don't really love me like I love you, and recently I have just met a guy that I think I can fall for..."

Special lies for women

"Tonight is a safe time for me....."

"It is that time of the month."

"Why didn't you tell me that sooner? After you called me, I jumped into a taxi and came right here!"

"Oh, I see. Are you saying that if we can't do 'that,' then it isn't worth getting together?"

—If you blame it on your period, most men have no choice but to go along with it.

"Hey! You did something different with your hair, didn't you? How come? Is something going on?"

"I thought that short hair might be nice for a change. Someone told me that. So, what do you think?"

"Is that some new boyfriend of yours saying that?"

"Well...."

—When you change boyfriends, do you change your hairstyle? So it seems. But even a woman without a boyfriend who changes her hairstyle often may be doing that as a symbol of a change of heart.

"It looks like I'm pregnant. You're going to be a father!"

"What! It must have been that time.... But didn't you say that it was a safe time?"

"That's what I thought too. This must be God's will. But you're happy about it, aren't you?"

"Well, sure...."

—If there is even a possibility that he is the father then it is difficult for him to deny it.

LIES THAT MEN TELL

Lies about time
• To a woman who is late

"That's okay. I was wondering if I had gotten the day wrong myself. I also thought that maybe I had the time off by an hour and I was getting worried. Well, these things happen. Anyway, I'm just glad that you came."

"I just happened to get here too early...."

"As soon as I saw your face, I totally forgot how long I'd been waiting...."

"Usually I make it a point not to wait over 15 minutes for someone no matter what, but today I waited 40 minutes for you! I just couldn't make myself leave...."

—Rather than getting upset about a woman being late, it is far better, if you really like her, to use it as a chance to show how much you care and how kind you are.

- **Using 'misunderstanding' as a reason for lateness**

"Boy, I'm really sorry I kept you waiting. I got on the wrong subway and was waiting on Platform 5 all this time instead of 3."

—If you get the timing right, saying that you misunderstood directions can be a good excuse.

- **Excuse for coming home late**

"I'm sure that I told you two or three days ago that I'd be entertaining an important client tonight and would be home late. That's strange. Well, if I forgot to mention it, I'm really sorry."

"A fax came in out of the blue from Singapore and all hell broke loose. They had some kind of breakdown with the machinery there and I had to ask Ms. Amamiya to stay late as well, so I ended up giving her a ride home."

—If you give the woman's name right out front, even a "dangerous excuse" now has the ring of truth to it.

- **Alibi of time**

"You're home awfully late (middle of the night) for someone who was supposedly playing golf."

"Yeah, well..... One of the guys I was golfing with made a hole-in-one. You know what happens then. We had to have this big celebration, and even after we got back to Shinjuku, we had to stop at a bar, and then another one.... No way to get out of that one."

—You can use golf to cover your fooling around if you make sure that the time frame is consistent with what you are claiming to be doing.

Say it without saying it
- **To approach someone**

"Haven't we met somewhere before? I know we have. The minute I met you I felt something close, like you were my little sister or something...."

"What? You live in Kichijoji? That's the same direction that I live in. Let me give you a ride home in a taxi with me."

—Even if you have never met her before, and even if you really live in the opposite direction, a light approach like this will seem very natural.

- **When you want to take the relationship further**

"I never give out the number of my own private phone to anyone, but I'm giving it to you!"

"The moment I saw you I knew that you and I were destined for something special."

• **Proposals**

"I keep having these dreams about you where you are my wife. You must have been wishing for that and subconsciously conveyed that to me. Let's make my dream come true..."

"If you say 'no' to me I won't be able to go on living. I can't imagine life without you."

—If you overexaggerate this point then you can avoid the casual "no" that comes from a casual proposal.

• **When you want to escape from accusations of unfaithfulness**

"Believe me, I am not the type of guy who just fools around with any available woman. If I were going to cheat on you, it would be the end of our relationship. That just isn't going to happen!"

—The woman probably doesn't want to absolutely break up either, so it is an excellent technique to say it strongly enough so that she won't pursue it any more than this.

• **For birthdays**

"If I were to be born again I'd want to still be married to you."

—This kind of well worn line may get a reaction of "yeah, right" but underneath it women are happy to hear such a line.

Telephone lies

"What? Are you sure we were getting together then? I'm really sorry, I totally forgot about it."

—If it is over the phone you can carry off this old-fashioned line of "totally forgetting."

- **Excuse for being late**

"Oh, the manuscript for your company? I gave that to my wife this morning to mail to you. I'm sure you'll get it tomorrow or the day after at the latest."

—Even if you really haven't sent it off, if you are just a day or so late, you can say "it's been sent" and thus pacify the other person.

"I'm working really hard on it right now. Take a look. I'm surrounded with the materials and I can hardly move for all the books here. Just give me two more days. I'll have it done for sure."

—If you explain in detail where you are and what is going on, it appears more truthful.

- **To prove that you aren't at home when you really are**

"I'm in Niigata on a business trip. I'm a little tired so I came back early to my hotel room to call you. I really miss you. I wish I could see you tonight. I'll be back late tomorrow, so we can get together the day after that. Bye...."

—If you are dating a few women at once, it is

wise to make a phone call like this before you have another woman come to your apartment.

• **Not there? Messages on answering machines**
"What?! You left a message cancelling on my machine? I didn't get it."

—If you insist strongly that you "didn't get the message" then they can't come up with any words to retort back to you.

At a night club
• **To a popular hostess**
"A really 'fine' woman says to a man that 'I'd go to bed with you' even if she has other special customers, and gives him that feeling of promise in the air. In that respect, you are really 'fine.' I'm always hoping..."

"If I was to say that I'm going to die tomorrow and this is the last day I'll ever see you, would you treat me specially?"

"These days I keep dreaming about you. And you're always naked in my dreams. But when I reach out for you, you always disappear! Even though I keep wanting you to stay until the end...."

—In "adult conversation" it is hard to know what is really true and what is really a lie.

• **To a woman chasing after a single man**
"Do I look like I have kids? I look older than I am, what a shame. And I'm really only 29. Well, at this age one out of three men are already married

EAST SIDE BOOKS
BISHOP, CA
THANK YOU

*   *

****

08-16-2005   MC #:0011

BOOKS   *14.00T1
BOOKS   *7.00T1
                            *1.63T1

TOTAL   *22.63
CASH   *22.63

          PM 3-07   0027
DON'T FORGET TO READ
*******SU RECIBO*********
*******GRACIAS**********
****
****

THE ART OF LYING

and have kids. Well, I get sick of being asked that so
I just say, "Yeah, I have one kid."

—Even if they are married and have kids, there
are many men who pretend to be single.

Lies to make invitations

"I promise I won't 'do anything,' so why don't
you come over to my apartment?"

"I don't want to leave you tonight. The gods are
telling me 'not to let you go...'"

"It is fate for us to be together. So let's seal our
fate together tonight."

"But I know you said we'd have breakfast too."

—Even though women know it is a lie, they
have a weak spot for these forceful seductions.

"I'm in a real hurry today, but let's just stop for
awhile at that hotel."

—If you use something extremely forceful like
this, an unexpected number of women will end up
saying yes.

Lies in bed
  • **If you are both single**

"You're beautiful. You are the only woman
for me. I can't think of any other woman but
you...."

—Sounds ridiculous. But even this kind of line
will give a woman an increased feeling of self-respect and make her feel really good.

- **Casual sex**

"Was it good for you? It was great for me. We are really good in bed together. We are totally compatible."

"I just can't get enough of you. If we were to ever be separated, I'd be really down. And if you ever got sick of me..."

—Even if you two are just fooling around with each other, it is a good idea to appear to be taking it seriously.

- **To your wife of seven years**

"They say that if you do it too much, then you get burnt out. I'd like to do it everyday, but let's take it slow. We have the rest of our lives...."

"No matter how wonderful that I think you are, I am totally bogged down at work and sometimes it kills my desire for you. If I try to make love to you now, I might really become impotent. You know, they say that these days there are more and more couples going without sex...."

—When you have a woman on the side, and your wife isn't satisfied with how often you are having sex, you may need to come up with a number of convincing excuses.

When drinking

"Last night I might have told you some secrets about people at work. I can't remember anything. I was really drunk and probably didn't get everything right. So please don't tell anyone what I said!"

"I know I made that promise to you, but at the time I was really drunk and I don't remember it at all."

—You may be able to explain it off to your boss, but you may also pay a high price.

"Everyone says that when you are drunk the real truth comes out, so I just pretend to be drunk and then tell lies."

Lies to say no
• **Saying no to an invitation to be in a relationship**

"It's like a dream to have a beautiful woman like you be interested in me. You may think I'm lying, but actually I have a fiancee back in Sendai. We've know each other since we were kids...."

"This is really too bad. It is truly unfortunate. Right now I am so busy putting in overtime that even though I really want to be with you, I just can't find the time anywhere. It looks like I really can't for awhile. I'm really sorry."

—If you want to be a popular guy, at the very least, you have to be able to turn a woman down without hurting her feelings.

• **Invitations from your boss**

"I'd love to go with you, but the fact is that I've already promised to go out drinking with friends. Would it be okay if they came too?"

—The important point is to mention your

friends. Your boss probably isn't asking you to go with him just because he wants to go drinking, but has something else in mind as well. He'll probably just suggest doing it another time.

• **Invitations from friends**

"Darn, if you'd asked me a little earlier I might have been able to."

"What? Thursday? If it was Wednesday I could do it...."

• **Turning down an invitation for bed**

"What rotten luck! For you to invite me today of all days.... Tomorrow morning I have to be up by 5 AM to go golfing with a really important client."

"Well, I'm a little embarrassed to admit this, but recently I have been having back trouble and I just can't do anything, well, strenuous... I'm sorry."

—If you're telling a lie to get out of going to bed with someone, then obviously you have no interest in them. All you need to do is find a reason that won't hurt their feelings.

Breaking up

• **With a woman you've been with for a long time**

"I want to pour my all into this work I'm doing now. I just can't get married right now. It isn't right to ask you to wait years and years for me. Please try to understand..."

- **Having an affair with someone without having to spend the night**

"I really wish that I could spend the night, but my wife is beginning to get suspicious. If she were to find out that I spent the night here, I think she would never agree to getting a divorce. So please just let me go now and put up with this for a little while longer."

- **To a girl you just sleep with**

"I really don't want to break up. But somewhere inside of me is a voice telling me that what we are doing is wrong. That voice keeps telling me that we have to call this off."

"I thought when we started this affair that you might burn out first. Now I wonder if I'm the one who's burning out. It is hard to break up, but maybe it's inevitable."

"All the other men you know are probably much better than me. I hope you'll be really happy with your next boyfriend..."

"Hiroko, I will never forget you till the day I die. I don't really know why it is that we are breaking up—it's just what I have to do..."

—These seem very pretentious and obvious lies. You need to be a good actor to carry them off.

- **When you want to break up a difficult relationship for good**

"I've put up with your emotional outbursts, trickery, fooling around for way too long. This is it for us. I feel sorry for the poor guy that you end up with next...."

—In order to make sure that you really break it off, you have to keep lying viciously and relentlessly. Acting like you are really fed up is an advanced technique.

• **When you don't want to hurt her**

"I thought that you and I would be a great couple.... But this is all my fault. I really don't want to break up. I still care for you...."

—A caring man tries not to hurt a woman when he breaks up with her. But if you are too good at this you will end up hurting her more, so be careful.

Lies with tears

MIHO: "Masao, you think that I don't know you were over at Azusa's place, don't you."

MASAO: (Has tears in his eyes) "...."

MIHO: (at last, unable to remain silent) "I can't believe you are crying. I'm sorry I doubted you."

MASAO: "I love you so much... How come you don't know that?"

—Since crying is so much less common for a man, this is a convincing way to be forgiven for many transgressions.

Not saying anything

• **When you are accused of cheating**

"What! Me, fool around?! Did you actually see

me fooling around? Who told you that kind of thing? I am absolutely not cheating on you."

—Even if you are cheating on her, as long as there is no witness, you are safe if you just keep denying it. But there is a limit to this....

—At times, the best policy is silence. If you do get caught, you should just keep your mouth shut. If you say too much it may just add fuel to the fire.

Lies of laughter

"Ha ha ha. That is really funny. Why would I have to lie about that. Ha ha ha."

"Ha ha ha. How in the world do these ridiculous stories get started?"

"People are so silly, ha ha...."

—This is in contrast to lies of keeping quiet. But for a man it may be difficult to laugh things off.

Lying about your age

"I heard that the Madame of the Club Manon was tricked by someone! That rich guy she's been going out with who claimed to be 75 is really just 60."

"How come he is adding 15 years to his age?"

"He knows that Madame is after his money when he dies. So he figured that she'd go for him more if he claimed to be older. If he was only 60 she wouldn't pay him any attention since he'd be around for awhile."

"And she can't very well complain that 'I've been tricked by my husband and he is too young'..."

Finding out your partner's feelings

"I'm going to have your baby...."

"That's a miracle! You know, I had a vasectomy three years ago. I wonder how this happened? There must be some mysterious phenomenon that modern science just can't explain..."

—Don't get excited and say "It's not mine" and don't deny it outright. It is better to see how she will react when you tell her this.

• **To a woman whose feelings you aren't sure of**

"Yesterday my boss called me over and told me that he was going to transfer me to Nagoya. What should we do?"

"My mother back home in Kyushu is pleading with me to come back there to live...."

—If the object is to find out her feelings, you can try this and then later say that your boss or mother changed their minds.

Special lies for men

"I want you to bear my child!"

"Really?"

"Have I ever lied to you?"

—Rather than coming up with the usual lines, it is better to use your male instinct and be straightforward.

"I've been to see the doctor and he tells me that I have prostrate trouble. I keep having to go to the bathroom. I knew there was something wrong...."

—If you need an excuse for not having sex with your wife, you can use "male illnesses" as an excuse.

"I can't believe anything you say anymore. You're such a liar. You keep saying "let's go to a movie together" or "let's take a drive together" but you never actually take me anywhere."

—Men often say to each other "let's get together soon for a beer" or "let's play golf sometime" in conversation just as a greeting, but this kind of thing doesn't work with a woman! If you make a promise to go somewhere, she'll expect to go!

"I have been working so hard that I have done more work than the guys outranking me in the company. Now my boss is pissed off about it. This puts me in a bad position. But the upper echelon has its eye on me so things are bound to improve. I'm really going to get ahead in this company..... Will you marry me?"

—A man lives on his "pride." If you are going to brag, do it well.

OTHER CASES

Tell a lie with a joke

- **What color is the sun?**

"Do you know what color the sun is?"

"Well, now that I think of it, it is red, isn't it?"

"Yes, most Japanese will answer that it's red, but Europeans say that the sun is yellow. And Chinese

say that it is white. The Chinese flag even repre-
sents that!"

"You're kidding!"

"They say that when you've had sex all night
that on the next morning the sun appears as yellow
to you. Yeah, those Westerners must really go at it!"

"Really?"

• Does a man control a woman?

"Women are really strong. A man in Moscow
went into a bookstore and asked, 'Do you have the
book called *Men Control Women?*' and the clerk
said to him, "If you're looking for fantasy novels,
they are over there."

"Really? Are you sure it wasn't the section for
ancient history that he wanted?"

• Slogans

"You know how companies have slogans and
mottos? Well, this is a story about a stingy man and
his daughter. The daughter was even stingier than
her father and said to him, "I'm going to show you
the way to report back on how my honeymoon is
going in the cheapest way possible." She sent him a
telegram from Paris and it had just one word on
it— "TWA."

"You mean the airline? Why...?"

"The slogan of TWA is "In and Out" and "Every
Five Minutes.""

• **Models**

"You know the pictures of food that you see in magazines? Well, after they finish taking pictures of it, the photographers all get to eat it. But they say that no matter what famous cook prepared it that it doesn't taste as good after they have finished shooting it. They say that the camera steals the taste away."

"You're lying!"

"But it is the same thing with fashion models. On days when they've been photographed they say that their flavor is gone as well....."

"Really?"

At the office

• **New employees to the boss**

NEW EMPLOYEE: "Boss!!"

BOSS: "What?"

NEW EMPLOYEE: "You shouldn't be the boss!"

BOSS: "What?"

NEW EMPLOYEE: "The man at the top has to be a guy of impeccable character and devotion and of upright character. Isn't that what you have said?"

• **To your section chief when he accuses you of not showing him something**

".....No, I'm sure that I showed you this data before."

"Nope, you never have. Why are you trying to tell me that you've done something you haven't done?!"

"A month ago on April 13 we had a meeting in the main meeting room. The department chief Mr. Yoshikawa was there as well and I'm sure that I handed this data to you that day."

"What! Are you sure? Well, I was pretty sure that you hadn't, but maybe...."

—If you give an exact date and place, and say who was there, and state this strongly and confidently then your boss's conviction will start to crumble.

At the golf course
 • **The way to "praise someone to death"**

"Hey, you've changed your swing. It's really good. Have you been taking lessons from a golf pro or someone?"

"What? Is there really something different about it?"

"Oh yeah. It has definitely gotten better. And your grip is nothing like before, either."

"Really?"

"It's like you're a different person."

—In order to destroy a player on the other team, the way to do it is to praise them so much that they become excessively self-conscious. In the end his shots will start coming apart.

 • **Out of bounds**
(Kicking a ball outside of the OB line)

"Hey! Somebody get over here and take a look. This is like a miracle. It isn't even 10 cm from the line. It is like the Goddess of Victory is smiling down on me. And I thought for sure that this was out of bounds..."

—Even a gentleman, if nobody is looking, will give into the "devil's temptation." However, the Goddess of Victory's smile is rarely there for someone who fakes a score.

Covering the truth with a joke

WOMAN: "There is another man I'm attached to. Recently I went out to dinner with him and...."

(Man who really cared for her): "What? Is this for real?"

WOMAN: "Just kidding..."

—If the man looks like he's going to get really angry by these words then you'd better be a little careful.

Getting at the truth

"You're lying to me! Yuta isn't really interested in me. I'm not his type, and believe me I would never go after another woman's man. You've got to believe me!"

—Most women tell lies, but if they get angry and are strongly denying it, then on the contrary, you may be able to see the real truth.

"You think that I have a hidden boyfriend?! And you say it is Mr. Yamamoto in the business section? Well, if that was true I'd be overjoyed!"

"It is a total lie. I mean, I'd love to say that Mr. Oda and I have something going on. But I can't tell a lie about it..."

—If you kind of confirm someone's statement in a joking way first, it is easier for the other person to believe the denial that comes after that.

Even though you know

"They say that love hotels these days have gotten really luxurious. I sure wish I could take a look just once. So tell me, is there a good one in Shinjuku?"

—When you want to ask something that is difficult to ask, it is good to pretend to be really innocent.

What you say and what you feel are different

"You are such a liar..."

"What! Why do you say that?"

"You tell me that you like me more than anyone else, but then you aren't making any moves on me at all..."

"That's because I promised not to do anything."

"Well, that just ends up hurting me more. You just don't understand anything, do you?"

"But you were the one who made me promise not to do anything if we came here..."

A lie at the spur of the moment
- **When a woman's handkerchief is found**

WIFE: "Whose handkerchief is this that I found in the pocket of your jacket? It even has lipstick on it. Explain to me just exactly what this is doing here! Are you trying to get back at me?"

HUSBAND: "What?! A woman's handkerchief? I have no idea. I'd like to know where it came from myself. I mean, I was really drunk last night. I can't remember at all...."

—Well, since it is the spur of the moment and you have no time to think, just try to stay calm and escape by pretending innocence.

- **When you are seen by a colleague on a secret date**

"Wow, what a coincidence! I just ran into Ms. Tanaka, and now you. So, where are you headed? After running into Ms. Tanaka this way we decided to drop by a bar...."

—It depends on where you are caught whether you can pull this off or not, but "blaming it on co-incidences" works best in a case like this.

- **When your wife answers the phone when your lover calls**

WIFE: "Who was that woman on the phone? She seemed awfully confused when I answered the phone."

HUSBAND: "Well, her name is Sato Chiyomi and she is in the business department of our company, but actually she is our director Mr. Yoshino's girl-friend. The director has asked me to be the "mes-senger" between them, and I just couldn't say no..."

"I got a call from Mrs. Yamashita, the wife of a guy in our section, and she says she wants to ask my advice about her husband. I think something seri-ous is going on.... If she's calling her husband's boss at home like this she must be pretty upset..."

—If you are going to tell a lot of lies, don't get them mixed up and keep track of what you say so that you don't have to pile lie upon lie. Stay calm and do it as naturally as you can.

A *backhanded lie*

"...You probably think that I am making this whole thing up. Nobody may believe it. But it is ab-solutely true. I know it may sound surprising...."

"If you think I'm lying, take a trip to Kyushu and check it out. You may find it hard to believe, but it is really true."

"Okay, if you don't want to believe me then just don't. I could care less if you do or don't..."

—If you affirm the "doubting heart" of the other person you can use that to your advantage. He may start to think, "Well, maybe it is true..."

Covering a lie

WIFE: "Oh, you're back. You were in Niigata on a business trip yesterday, right? Well, yesterday at lunch time I got a call from your office from Mr.

Tanabe who said he needed to get a hold of you right away on urgent business. Explain that!"

HUSBAND: "Mr. Tanabe? Yeah. Well, that trip I was on was kept confidential from the other sections. That's why he didn't know. Anyway, how did our son do on that test he had to take? I've been worrying about his results...."

—When your lie is about to be discovered, it is smart to quickly change topics to one that the other person is very involved with and escape that way.

A group lie

(When a group of friends is gathered)

ICHIRO: "So what's going on between you and Kazuya anyway? Are you a couple or not? From a man's point of view he is a really great catch. He's sure to get ahead at work..."

SAORI: "Do you think so?"

KENJI: "No mistake about it. He's a hard worker and sincere. He's a quiet guy, so a lot of women don't see his good points...."

TAKESHI: "Yeah. You don't see it at first with him, but he's the type that is really going to succeed..."

—When a group of men gets together and all praise one guy to a woman then it is easy to get the woman who is still unsure about a guy to firm up her feelings. This is an advanced tactic. Naturally this can be used in the opposite way as well, to discourage her from seeing him.

Postscript—
TRUE WISDOM

What must a person know in order to live both gracefully and comfortably? The key to making your way through the nineties is not in literal truth, but in "true wisdom." Honesty requires a great deal of stamina. A person who is completely open and honest is also easily wounded. And in the end, we all know that a person who always works hard and is sincere is not necessarily rewarded.

It is a most difficult feat to convey the truth through words. The vast majority of patients seen at psychiatric clinics are sincere and serious hardworking people. However, when their sincere efforts go unrecognized, they come to an impasse and are unable to cope. When they are unable to find another path, or just take a break and rethink the situation, they come to the clinic complaining of being depressed or feeling frustrated.

When a couple visits the clinic wanting to revitalize their marriage, I tell them, "Your earnestness is causing the problem." Changing your viewpoint is the trick to solving the problem.

I often see mothers loaded down with guilt over childrearing and worrying about where they have gone wrong. I tell these women, "Children will thrive on their own. Just let them be and step away from them." Even so it is hard for them to change what they believe.

It is easy to get bogged down when you are entangled in a number of problems. You begin to wonder just how you can ever extricate yourself from them! The answer is to learn how to lie well. Just use a lie and say something that you know very well is not true to the people around you, and even to yourself. We have all been taught since childhood that one should be diligent and sincere, and put forth our best efforts at all times. But unfortunately, effort and sincerity alone will not help us to lead life easily in our society. If a problem can be solved easily then extra effort is not necessary. If you can get along well at work and with your partner, then why hold on to sincerity as a symbol alone?

One lie may save a person's life and just a very small lie can help human relationships of all kinds run more smoothly.

People who are "sincere" or "hardworking" are sometimes the most unaccomodating and stubborn people around! Few of us realize that. People who are unable to change their attitude and insist on the utmost sincerity are causing the most aggravation and trouble to the people around them. No wonder it is often said that, "The less wisdom a person has, the more sincere and harder working they will try to be." Thus, what we believe to be common sense or knowledge today is often wrong.

In this book, I speak to people who are so caught up in the problems around them, they feel there is no escape. The people I address this book to are:

- Serious and sincere people who continue to find themselves unsuccessful

- People who are unable to take control of their own lives

- People who are unsatisfied with their relations with others

I have tried here to teach ways to use lies skillfully. A lie can be a remedy for life. In addition, when one goes beyond a lie and the common truth to "true wisdom," the real truth becomes clear.

It would make me very happy if this book should be of use to all people who feel troubled.

April, 1996
Sakai Kazuo